# Internet Communication
# in Six Classrooms:
## Conversations Across Time, Space, and Culture

# Internet Communication in Six Classrooms:
## Conversations Across Time, Space, and Culture

Ruth Garner
Mark G. Gillingham
University of Illinois at Chicago

**LEA** LAWRENCE ERLBAUM ASSOCIATES, PUBLISHERS
1996  Mahwah, New Jersey

Lawrence Erlbaum Associates
10 Industrial Avenue
Mahwah, New Jersey 07430

**Library of Congress Cataloging-in-Publication Data**

Internet communication in six classrooms : Conversations
across time, space, and culture / Ruth Garner and Mark G.
Gillingham
      p. cm.
Includes biographical references and indexes.
ISBN 0-8058-2275-5 (pbk. : alk. paper)
1. Education—Computer network resources—Case
studies. 2. Internet (Computer network)—Case studies.
3. Communication in education—Case studies. I. Gillingham, Mark G. II. Title.
LB1044.87.G37 1996
025.06'37—dc20                  96-31862
                                 CIP

Printed in the United States of America
10  9  8  7  6  5  4  3  2  1

# Contents

# Foreword

## Bertram C. Bruce

When Robert Taylor brought together the now classic collection, *The Computer in the School: Tutor, Tool, Tutee*[1], he felt compelled to write about "the chaotic range of activities" included within the realm of computing and education (p. 2) . The articles in that collection, originally published between 1965 and 1980, described roles for the computer that ranged from the *expert*, which presents well-organized material on a particular topic, to the *assistant,* which carries out calculations or edits a text, to the *student* that learns from its human tutor. Even among a small set of authors, there was a wide diversity of visions about what computing in the schools might or should become.

Now, roughly 2 decades later, it is worthwhile to reflect on how classroom use of computers has evolved. Following the evolutionary metaphor, we might ask whether Taylor's "chaotic range" was analogous to the rapid speciation that occurs when organisms are introduced into new ecosystems. How did these species evolve? Are particular ones surviving in greater numbers and spreading to new locales? What are the trends; where are we headed? What is technology in the classroom becoming?

This book by Ruth Garner and Mark G. Gillingham does not promise any grand evolutionary tale, but was written only to "tell half a dozen stories . . . about teachers and students who . . . are able to move ideas . . . across time, space, and culture" (p. xiii). Each story is particular and hardly typical. A quick look at Kathy Nell's World Wide Web site tells anyone that her classroom's use of computers goes far beyond the ordinary, or what anyone could, in good conscience, ask a teacher to do. Kathy Plamondon's

---

[1]Taylor, R. P. (1980). *The computer in the school: Tutor, tool, tutee.* New York: Teachers College Press.

KIDCAFE opens up classroom communication in ways proscribed in many classrooms. Daniel Wilcox and Hugh Dyment find ways to expand the communication possibilities for both themselves and their high school students, just as Ruth Coleman and Chris Meier do for their elementary school students. In fact, all six of these classrooms embody visions that both realize and extend the possibilities for computer-mediated communication in extraordinary ways.

Moreover, the classrooms are atypical when considered independent of their computer practices. The obvious cases are those of Chris Meier and Hugh Dyment, who teach in Tununak, Alaska, a village with only 325 people. But one could also say, without in any way diminishing the hard work and creativity the teachers have shown, that each teacher is unusual in having found supports that many other teachers do not find, from parents, researchers, an administrator, the community, Learning Circles, or people on the Internet.

But as soon as we attempt to specify how these classrooms are special, we are made to confront the question of what a typical classroom would be. What constitutes the typical group of students, the typical teacher, the typical set of resources? What is the typical sociocultural context for learning? The stories here show why the typical classroom is chimerical, both in the sense of being imaginary and in the sense that if we were to find it, we would undoubtedly discover that it is a unique and fascinating creature representative of only itself. As these teachers and students work to define what technology means for their classrooms, they find themselves drawing on their own histories, using the technology to amplify who they are and what they value. The details would vary greatly between one of these classrooms and any other we might pick, just as they vary among the six classrooms. But the process of constituting the technology through situation-specific practices is a constant.

Beyond this, the situations of classrooms do have much in common. Garner and Gillingham highlight these similarities when they identify patterns in the Internet communication—the telling of stories, the maintenance of social relations, the naturalizing of technology, and the importance of teachers. These are patterns in any classroom, which are simply realized in distinctive ways and, perhaps, expanded, through Internet communication.

Thus, despite having only six cases, and special ones at that, this book does far more than it promises. Yes, it tells intriguing stories, with wonderful examples of students' writing. But it also begins to answer those questions about where classroom computing is evolving and what it might become. It provides a multifaceted answer that might be surprising, especially to the familiar, but contradictory claims that the computer is either a revolutionizing force or only a passing fad.

One facet that I see in their answer is that we cannot talk of just the computer's role, as Taylor (1980) did (and as I have done in other works). The computer-mediated communication we see here is not simply added to the classroom like a school assembly program. It is deeply embedded in the value systems and social practices of the students and teachers. When Meier's Yup'ik students write, they construct e-mail as an opportunity to tell about their families, to build the connections through kinship that can form the foundation for further conversation, as they know from oral interactions. This is not the e-mail constructed in the corporate world or even in most other classrooms. Indeed, Meier's suggestion to edit the messages reflects his awareness that e-mail is a different technology in other settings and that shorter messages would promote the intercultural communication they seek. But then Garner and Gillingham point out that the editing may deny aspects of the children's language and cultural identity.

The discussion is a fascinating one and I doubt that any of the participants, children or adults could be totally confident about any prescription for this classroom, much less for another setting. But what is clear is that the very conception of what e-mail is for, how it should be used, and what role it has in the classroom, cannot be separated from the teacher's pedagogical goals, the cultural norms prevailing in the classroom and surrounding community, or the student's purposes for writing. E-mail, the tool, does not come into the classroom with its role and uses predetermined, but rather is assimilated into daily practices. That's one reason the approach taken here is so important: It seeks to make sense of the daily life of six classrooms, in which Internet communication is just one integral part.

A related facet of the answer these stories provide is that we need to reconsider what we mean when we say that a particular technology is in use in a classroom. These classrooms have moved very far from the ideas of programmed instruction or the book on a computer. But what technology are they using? We can say "Internet communication," and if we did not have the richness of the six stories before us, that might prove satisfactory. But as soon as we begin to enter into the diverse and complex worlds of these classrooms, we see that Internet communication itself has diverse and complex meanings.

To take just one example out of many, when Tununak teenagers in Dyment's class use e-mail to talk with adults who have left the village, their experience of schooling is expanded beyond any simple notion of developing writing skills. To say that they are using e-mail or a file transfer program might be technically correct, but would trivialize the profound meaning that this "conversation between equals" can have. Moreover, that sort of conversation has very different personal and pedagogical implications from the intercultural exchanges between Garner's and Gillingham's classes or the teacher to teacher dialogue between Dyment and Meier. These examples make abundantly clear that an account of technology in terms of circuits and processors alone is sorely lacking. We have to have the kinds of detailed and sensitive accounts that stories like these provide if we are to understand what the technology is and what it means for education.

A third facet of the answer that I noted, and the book provides many more, is how this close look at technology, with its emphasis on the Internet, the World Wide Web, e-mail, virtual communities, and so on, brings us ineluctably back to questions of teaching, learning, thinking, communicating, and caring. The strengths and weaknesses of computer-mediated communication have little to do with technical features of the new technologies. It is true, of course, that being able to easily share texts across time and space creates possibilities for sharing across cultures that were not afforded previously. But the fascinating exchanges recounted here arose when teachers allowed students to write about things that mattered to them and when teachers worked hard to support students' learning. And the limits many educators have encountered are not primarily in the technical realm.

This is why when we ask about what's happening with new information and communication technologies in the schools we find the question is not so simple as it seems. We can look to see how many schools are connected to the Internet, but it is much more difficult to see whether and how students' and teachers' lives are changed. To do the latter, we find ourselves inquiring into social relations, political values, and teaching goals, not just modem rates. Garner and Gillingham tell us stories that provide contexts for those inquiries. Thus, they show in a beautifully written book that the question about computers is ultimately a question about ourselves.

# Preface

This is a book about communication. We tell half a dozen stories about teachers and students who, because of recent advances in telecommunications, are able to move ideas back and forth across time, space, and culture. We attempted to tell the stories in a manner that makes them accessible and useful to both the scholarly community and classroom teachers.

We think that classroom telecommunications activity is quite remarkable, not because of the possibility of electronic "handshaking" and rapid movement of bits of information via Internet technology, but because of the intensely social activity that the technology supports. We find it remarkable, for instance, that young children learn to provide enough detail to make unfamiliar ideas comprehensible to other children thousands of miles away, and that adolescents are able to tailor their language so that it is informal and engaging and still useful in persuading peers of the greater legitimacy of one of two competing claims. It is also remarkable, we think, that teachers swap accounts of classroom triumphs and failures—and even discuss basic beliefs about teaching and learning—with relative strangers.

Each of the six stories that we tell makes it clear that teachers and students are attempting to connect, often across considerable geographic and cultural distance. They are informing, entertaining, and persuading and, as they use computers to accomplish all sorts of social purposes, they belie the stereotype of computer users as isolates relating to machines but not to other people.

The connections made are both similar to and different from non-electronic connections. Many of the conversations—full of wit, intimacy, grace, fear, bias, and joy—could have occurred on the playground or at the mall. What is quite different, however, is that children in Joliet, IL seldom meet Yup'ik Eskimo children on the playground, and adolescents going to the mall near rural La Center, WA rarely meet peers with a wide range of experiences and diverse views on topics such as gays in the military or evolution. Teachers, who spend most of their days in splendid isolation from other adults, seldom find colleagues with whom they can talk openly about teaching. Children, adolescents, and adults have an opportunity to have contact on the Internet with persons whom they simply would not encounter otherwise. As Fred Newmann (1991) reminded us, it can be a formidable cognitive task to encounter someone else's experiences indirectly and attempt to understand him or her. Each of the teachers in this book is providing extended opportunities for students to learn to do just that.

Who are the six teachers? Ruth Coleman (chapter 2) is a Joliet, IL elementary teacher who raised four sons and then returned to college to prepare to teach. Chris Meier (chapter 3) is in only his second year of teaching fifth and sixth graders in the tiny Yup'ik Eskimo village of Tununak, AK. Hugh Dyment (chapter 4), Chris's colleague in Tununak, teaches high school classes in the village. Kathy Plamondon (chapter 5) is a first-year teacher of seventh graders in the poor, mostly rural district of La Center, WA. Daniel Wilcox (chapter 6) is a seasoned high school teacher in Santa Maria, CA; he tries to hook adolescents on literature and has recently been hooked himself by computer networking possibilities. Finally, Kathy Nell (chapter 7)—a teacher in the Philadelphia school system for 23 years—has this year created a World Wide Web site where her fourth-grade students publish their work and browse for information.

Each is a quite extraordinary teacher working in a rather ordinary setting. Their conversations about conceptions and actions, their reflections about their own practice, sit at the core of this book. Each teacher has agreed to continue conversations with us, with each other, and with readers: E-mail and Web addresses are noted in the list of contributors.

# ACKNOWLEDGMENTS

We acknowledge our enormous debt to the teachers, who have taught us a great deal about teaching and learning. We also acknowledge very helpful suggestions from Naomi Silverman, our editor at Lawrence Erlbaum Associates, Inc. and from the reviewers whom she recruited to read our manuscript—Victoria Chou, Sally M. Oran, David Reinking, Suzanne Wade, and James D. Williams. Finally, we thank Judy Thompson and Karla Bellingar, both at Michigan State University, who have provided invaluable technical assistance.

*Ruth Garner*
*Mark G. Gillingham*

# List of Contributors

**RUTH COLEMAN**, Joliet, IL
ruthc423@aol.com

**HUGH DYMENT**, Tununak, AK
hughdym@aol.com

**RUTH GARNER**, Chicago, IL
rgarner@uic.edu

**MARK G. GILLINGHAM**, Chicago, IL
markgill@uic.edu

**CHRIS MEIER**, Tununak, AK
cdmeier@aol.com

**KATHY NELL**, Philadelphia, PA
http://www.philsch.k12.pa.us/schools/
forrestelem/Class308.4.html

**KATHY PLAMONDON**, La Center, WA
kathykp@teleport.com

**DANIEL WILCOX**, Santa Maria, CA
seaquaker@aol.com

# I

## Introduction

# 1

# Introduction to Internet Conversations As Intensely Social Activity

Why should we tell stories about classrooms? Madeleine Grumet (1987) reminded us that telling stories, even to close friends or colleagues, is always risky business: Listeners wait for our story to end so that theirs can begin, and they often focus on the wrong parts, the parts that matter least to us. They recall the stories that we would have them forget, but forget the ones that we most want them to remember.

Yet there is no better form, we have decided, for describing events that occur over time in a classroom. We tell half a dozen stories in this book about what Philip Jackson (1990) called "the everyday affairs of educational practitioners and those they serve" (p. 7), each one in some way touching on the use of new technology to connect teachers and students in one classroom to teachers and students in another classroom.

Each story is about a particular context—a classroom, a teacher, and a group of students—and also about what Marshall McLuhan (1964, p. 93) called "the global village." We live in a global village because transportation advances allow us to move, and technological advances allow our ideas to move, both producing significant contact across cultures. McLuhan's notion of a global village may be even more powerful than he realized: Three decades ago, television moved ideas in one direction, but today, advances in telecommunications allow ideas to move back and forth across time, space, and culture. It is this new movement of ideas that particularly interests us.

**3**

We are the narrators, not the actors, in these six stories. We derive principles from the set of stories that we tell. In this introductory chapter, we explain a bit about case methods, about why we told these stories rather than others that we might have told. We also discuss telecommunications technology and the intensely social activity that it supports.

# WHAT IS A CASE?

A case is a story—a "true" story based on actual events. Because they are stories, cases have narrative elements: setting (in ours, a set of classrooms observed for a single school year), characters (in this book, teachers and students), and plot (in these cases, classroom events, especially communication events).

However, a case is also more than a story. Lee Shulman (1992) said that to call something a case is to make a theoretical claim—a claim that the story told is one instance in a category. In other words, it is a case *of something,* meriting consideration for its particularity, but also for the category that it represents. Our stories are all about connecting, about building community, about communicating over many miles. There is considerable diversity among the cases (a classroom in Philadelphia and one in a tiny Eskimo village on the Bering Sea, very experienced teachers and a first-year teacher, fourth-grade students and students getting ready to finish high school, student-to-student correspondence and multistudent discussions on an international e-mail list), but all of the cases are instances of communicating over considerable distance (the "of something," in Shulman's definition of a case).

It is rather astonishing, is it not, that students in one classroom can send a message over the Internet to students in another classroom and have extended discussions, despite the fact that they have never seen one another and have never shared any face-to-face experiences? It does happen: Children and adolescents repeat one another's topics, use detail to make ideas familiar and memorable, and tailor their language to meet the needs of distant readers. They tell stories, ask questions, and present arguments to peers whom they do not know outside of the Internet exchanges.

If our cases are stories and instances, they are also sets of data to be analyzed. In describing what teachers do and say, we draw inferences about their instructional practice and, in describing what students do and say, we draw inferences about their literacy behaviors. The most important data in all of this are the *very words* of the teachers and students. The participants have given us permission to "eavesdrop" on their electronic conversations, and because the conversational records can be forwarded, stored, and retrieved with ease, the data are remarkably rich and inviting.

We are reminded by both Lee Shulman and Dona Kagan (1993) that, because we are narrators rather than actors in the cases, because we are using the data of Internet messages in an attempt to understand a communication phenomenon, we are presenting *case studies,* rather than case reports (first-person accounts of events) or teaching cases (original accounts prepared especially for instructional purposes). We have worked closely with the teachers in interpreting data—have been "sympathetic witnesses" to their practice, to use John Olson's (1988, p. viii) phrase. We fully expect that the cases will have value in teacher education and rhetoric classrooms. However, our primary purpose in crafting the case studies is to understand a communication phenomenon. The case study, which offers in-depth understanding of a context or set of contexts has, of course, had a long history in educational research, in clinical psychology and, as Harry Broudy (1990) reminded us, in the professions of law and medicine in which problems of practice are an important part of the canon.

## WHAT ASSUMPTIONS FOLLOW
## FROM A CHOICE OF CASE METHODS?

Jerome Bruner (1990) said that he believes stories always resist logical procedures for establishing what they mean, that they must be interpreted. Of course, this means that each story is open to diverse interpretations.

For instance, we are critical of second-year teacher Chris Meier for asking his students in Alaska to delete introductory segments of their messages to Illinois—sections that were consistent with the village practice of naming friends and family members in hopes of finding a person in common, but were sections that Chris anticipated would confuse the children in Illinois. We interpreted this decision as heavy-handed editing and as a lapse in consideration of his students' culture and context; however, another reader might applaud Chris for worrying about cross-cultural confusion and might interpret his action as sound instructional practice.

We assume that our interpretation of classroom events is but one possible interpretation. We include much raw data in this volume—actual words from teachers and (especially) from students—so that alternative interpretations are possible. Not only do the data invite alternative interpretations from different individuals, they also invite revision of interpretation from a single individual, for—as Gary Sykes and Tom Bird (1992) reminded us—cases can be revisited repeatedly.

Interpretation is linked to one's belief system, of course. In discussing that system, Suzanne Wade, Audrey Thompson, and William Watkins (1994) noted that it determines what we label "common sense," what we view as normal, relevant, or self-evident, and it influences, often profoundly, what we evaluate as "good" or "bad." We would not tell stories about communication events in classrooms if we were not interested in the topic. We have some rather strong beliefs about typical classroom discourse (it is too teacher-centered), about Internet discourse (it presents great possibilities for new forms of community, new opportunities for students to communicate across time, space, and culture), and about adoption of new technology in schools (buying hardware and software, but providing no ongoing on-site support to teachers, is a bad investment).

Given strong beliefs, we must guard against two errors of interpretation: First, we might present what Michael Connelly and Jean Clandinin (1990) called "the Hollywood plot," in which—as in many educational program-evaluation documents—everything works out well in the end because instances of failure of an innovation are excluded, whereas instances of success are included, all in the name of preserving narrative flow. Second, the opposite might occur, as Kathy Carter (1993) warned. We might create one-dimensional characters, focusing so narrowly on whether teachers fit our preconceptions of proficiency in $X$ (in this book, using Internet resources wisely and inventively) that we exclude all instances of enlightened practice in $Y$ and $Z$. A different narrator might focus on $Y$ (e.g., teaching mathematics for understanding) or on $Z$ (e.g., assessing text comprehension wisely) and might pronounce a "failed" teacher to be a star. Narrators are mostly invisible, as Carter noted, because of rhetorical convention, but the narrators (i.e., we) play a critical role in how richly and kindly our characters are viewed and presented to readers.

All of this is to say that whenever we tell a story about teachers and students, we impose structure and meaning on classroom events. Our stories are theories, markers to bundles of beliefs. We try on many occasions in these cases to note our intrusion in the telling of the stories—to be self-conscious about our analyses, as Susan Florio-Ruane (1987) advised—but we know full well that we noted some, not all, of the instances in which we intrude.

Another assumption of ours is that context is critical. Context is actually the whole point of cases. As Mary Lee Smith (1987) said about all qualitative methods, case studies among them, they are rooted in the notion of context sensitivity. If someone prepares a case study on a single teacher and group of students, he or she will inevitably be faulted by some positivistic scientists for bad sampling (why this teacher, these students, and not others?) and for related low generalizability (what can we possible conclude about the thoughts, beliefs, and actions of all teachers and students from the extended study of just one classroom?).

The conventional wisdom among researchers who use qualitative methods is that what is sacrificed in generalizability is compensated for by in-depth contextual information. Rather than textbook lists of decontextualized, general, impersonal principles about teaching and learning, cases present whole stories that are rich in contextualized, specific, personal information. Jerome Bruner (1990) chided us for ever thinking that human action of any sort could be fully and properly accounted for from just the inside out by reference only to dispositions, traits, learning capacities, and such. Action is situated within a cultural world.

So, of course teaching and learning are situated. They occur in a context—a complex one with multiple overlapping events. In telling a story about a particular classroom, we inevitably capture some events and leave others out. For instance, we make no claim at all to having adequately framed classroom events within the larger context of teachers' life histories.

As we noted elsewhere (Garner, 1990), there is some continuity across contexts, but there is also systematic difference. Teaching in a large city is not the same as teaching in a village of 325 located 300 miles from the nearest road. Learning to correspond on the Internet in one's first language is different from learning to correspond in one's second language. Having a dedicated phone line for modem use in one's own classroom and sending messages immediately is different from having to delay sending of messages by saving them on a floppy disk for your teacher to send by way of America Online (AOL) at home. As Bertram C. Bruce and Andee Rubin (1993) reminded us, we need to avoid the technocentric fallacy of seeing technology as a context-free innovation. The "same technology" is *not* the same in different classrooms. We assume, as did Lee Shulman (1992), that a set of cases, such as those in this book, is helpful. The collection tempers the impact of any single entry.

## THE INTERNET AS A CONTEXT

So, classrooms are contexts. The Internet is also a context, one that links the cases in this book. One of the most interesting aspects of the Internet discourse that we studied (apparent in all of the cases, so an instance of continuity) is that it differs so dramatically from typical classroom discourse. Carmen Luke, Suzanne de Castell, and Allan Luke(1983) described what occurs in many classrooms: Teachers teach texts (texts include games, films, workbooks, and worksheets), and student discourse is about the texts, based on the texts, or directed by the texts. Students learn early in their school careers that what is in the texts will most likely be on the test, and the texts establish boundaries for what topics can legitimately be discussed, what knowledge matters (what is "official knowledge," as Allan Luke [1995, p. 3] labeled it).

As for topics for writing, Sara Mosle's (1995b) description of what she did in her first year of teaching presents common practice:

> I would put a topic on the board—"What is your favorite movie?" or "What did you dream last night?"—and my students would invariably groan, "I don't want to write about that!" And who could blame them? Adults don't write in such a void. The purpose of writing—a business letter, a poem, even a bit of graffiti—is to communicate. But in my early, contrived lessons, my students weren't writing to anyone. (p. 53)

Courtney Cazden (1988) reminded us that for both speaking and writing in the classroom, it is the teacher who always responds, often in an evaluative way. In all speaking and writing assignments, no matter who the ostensible audience may be, the teacher's response is the one that counts.

The situation is radically different in Internet discourse. For one thing, the topics (at least in every instance that we know) are chosen by the students, linked to their knowledge and interest rather than to an authorized textbook's contents or a teacher's chalkboard list. Given the origin in the students themselves, the topics are what Sylvia Ashton-Warner (1986) described as "dynamic material" with intense meaning to students. Note the diversity in this partial list of topics from our cases:

adopting a baby in the family
AIDS
being accused of stealing by one's grandmother
a basketball tournament
Bill Clinton
changing schools
cold weather
confirmation class
crabbing

"dumb blonde" jokes
euthanizing unwanted dogs
evolution
a fire in the neighborhood
gays in the military
high school graduation
hockey
hunting ptarmigan
a local funeral
rundown schools
sleepovers
spitting on somebody's food
state troopers coming to town

A second element that distinguishes Internet discourse from typical classroom discourse is audience: Other students, not teachers, respond to students. When a topic really appeals, students many miles apart may write back and forth for weeks or even months, negotiating the difficult rhetorical territory of trying to figure out what their distant communication partners know and what more they should say on a variety of topics. Students may transform a question from one person into statements of their own (or the reverse). On an international e-mail list, a handful of students may try to persuade the others of a particular point of view, responding to arguments, point by point, over a series of messages. The students are connected to the discourse and to one another despite considerable distance between their classrooms.

The teacher's role in this activity (at least in our cases) is mostly advisory. For instance, Ruth Coleman, a fifth-grade teacher in Illinois, provided considerable support for the revising process at the beginning of the year, putting messages on the overhead projector and asking the class to work together to find likely trouble spots in structure or mechanics, but by year's end, most revision occurred at the computer, as children worked together on composing. Hugh Dyment's high school students in Alaska determined from the start when they would write on the Internet, to whom they would write, and what they would write, and peers acted as editors from the start of the year. Hugh's role was to assist his students when they requested help—usually in locating e-mail addresses. And, in the editing cycles in Kathy Nell's Philadelphia classroom, she shared editing responsibilities with fourth-grade authors, other students, and word processor tools.

Internet language represents an interesting genre—certainly not written language as we normally think about it, but not quite oral language either.

Quite some time ago, Andee Rubin (1980) attempted to distinguish between oral and written language. She noted that a person's oral language experiences are mostly interactive conversations in which the person participates as both speaker and listener. Participants share a spatial and temporal context, and their verbal communication is augmented by various forms of nonverbal communication, such as gesture. Written language experiences are also interactive, but the reader does not participate as writer except in the most extraordinary of instances (e.g., an editor sitting next to an author reviewing text and jotting down suggested modifications), and participants in written language experiences seldom share the same space and time.

These are important distinctions, but Gordon Wells and Gen Ling Chang-Wells (1992) may have been right when they said that the dichotomy between spoken and written language is not all that important educationally. They propose that we ask whether any language event, oral or written, contributes to sound thinking. From this perspective, writing is a means of giving a permanent representation to thoughts expressed in speech; by writing something down, we can use more ideas than we could ever possibly remember.

In Internet discourse, the distinction between spoken and written language is definitely blurred. There is permanent representation, for messages are stored as electronic data, and they can be retrieved (and thus analyzed by us) with ease. However, there are many conversational elements: involvement; almost time, if not space, in common because of the potential of quick response; effective substitutes for gesture (e.g., an *asterisk* or CAPS for emphasis); and an informal, interactive style in which "talk words" (e.g., "say," "tell," and "hear") appear frequently. We like to use Shirley Brice Heath's (1983) phrase "conversations written down" (p. 213) to describe Internet communication that we have read and analyzed.

We should note that we followed particular conventions in reproducing these conversations written down in this book. First, as we said, we reproduced the *very words* of teachers and students, never altering spelling, capitalization, or punctuation. If we reproduced only portions of a long message, an ellipsis always indicates that a portion of the original message was omitted. Bracketed text indicates a comment from us, rather than from the teachers or students. With their permission, we used the actual names of the teachers involved. In the case of students, with two exceptions, we used pseudonyms. The exceptions to this rule are (a) the international e-mail list for 10- to 15-year-olds, in which, because messages are archived (and, therefore, readily available in read-only mode to non-10- to 15-year-olds like us), we eliminated surnames but used actual first names of participants, and (b) the Web site work from Philadelphia, in which, because work is published (and thus available, with student names appended, to all Web browsers), we did not delete names.

# COMMUNICATION, TELECOMMUNICATIONS, AND SCHOOLS

The Internet is only the newest among many technologies introduced to schools. Educators have "enthused" over the years about a whole string of technologies—textbooks, educational television, computer-assisted instruction, and, most recently, microcomputers. Yet, much of the equipment that generates enthusiasm one year can be found the next year languishing in a school closet. Why?

One explanation is inadequate management of innovation. That is, new technology is often delivered haphazardly to classroom teachers. If there is a poor fit between what a new innovation can offer and the curriculum already in place, the technology is doomed to failure—if continuing use by teachers counts as success.

Teachers often can think of very meaningful ways in which to use technology when they are sufficiently prepared to do so, but it is common practice to announce arrival of unfamiliar equipment (sometimes only part of it) the week before school begins in the fall, to hire a consultant for a day-long workshop, and then abandon users to their own devices, with little or no on-site support. There may not even be a person in the building who can install equipment and keep it working properly. Daniel Wilcox, high school teacher in Santa Maria, CA (and strong advocate for Internet communication between classrooms) told us a very common tale of woe at the end of September: "Our school network was supposed to be up and running at the start of school, but they are still working on it, so I have been lugging my computer home most nights to go online and send the mail [from students in his classroom to high school students in Alaska]."

We have a different story about haphazard support that worries us just as much—a story about a university and the local schools. At Otto Middle School in Lansing, MI, a group of sixth-grade teachers and the school's media specialist formed a "tech team," meeting during one period a week for an entire school year to discuss telecommunications opportunities and needs. Otto Middle is a professional development school, affiliated with Michigan State University's College of Education, so the team had every right to assume that resources would be sufficient and assistance would be immediate, but that was hardly the case. It took many months to buy local area network and Internet equipment, secure accounts, and learn about capabilities. Both the university and the school district expressed support for Otto's Internet initiatives, but progress in getting authorization from the two huge bureaucracies to purchase equipment and accounts has been glacial.

Another explanation for minimal technology use, one that David Cohen (1988) favored, is presence of institutional disincentives to using new technology. Two disincentives are particularly important: enormous problems of subject-matter coverage (nudging teachers toward single textbooks and anthologies, not new technology) and substantial administrative pressure to keep classrooms "managed" (moving teachers to assign seatwork, not individual or small-group work on new computers).

In the classrooms we studied, it struck us immediately that in every case the *teacher*, not the building administrator or district curriculum specialist, initiated use of telecommunications in his or her classroom, so external mandates and bad match to curricular goals were not an issue. Similarly, in every case, the teacher (and students) told us that students enjoy Internet communication, so management of unruly behavior has not been a problem. (See the case of Kathy Plamondon's seventh-grade classroom for a more detailed discussion of the old progressive education maxim that students become engrossed in activities and topics in which they are deeply interested.)

What is there about telecommunications that accounts for both teachers and students liking it? We are convinced that the most important single reason why students enjoy this form of communication is that they are allowed, even encouraged, to communicate with other kids on topics of interest to kids (a basketball tournament, gays in the military, etc.). And, we are convinced that the most important reason why teachers celebrate the form is that students practice speaking and writing willingly—in a way that they do not when only they (the teachers) respond and when topics are prescribed. Students send messages eagerly and, as Daniel Wilcox reports, "are keenly disappointed" when they do not receive quick responses.

This is intensely social activity—quite different, as Batya Friedman (1991) noted, from popular views of a computer nerd as an isolate who relates to a machine, but not to other people. Children and adolescents can discuss interesting ideas with other children and adolescents (even with adults), crossing cultural, economic, and regional boundaries while they do so. In this regard, very new technology supports very old goals of communication and community. There is an electronic component, but at the heart of telecommunications is the same human need to connect that one hears in conversations on the playground or at the mall.

Precursor to telecommunications is the set of pen-pal systems, which have been received by students reasonably well over the years. In these systems also, there is authentic writing from kids to kids on kid-selected topics. There is a nontrivial difference, however, and that lies in potential speed of response. When a student wants desperately to get his or her idea "out there" or to hear how well an idea has already been received, Internet communication (but not pen-pal systems) can offer response times of minutes, not days or weeks. So, Erica can send a short message to the international e-mail list for 10-to 15-year-olds:

> Hi my name is Erica. Clinton is such a dweeb. It's hard to believe he's a president. My dad calls him slick willy. My dad hates him thats why. Who do you want to be are president . . .

And Allen can write back within hours, advising Erica to think for herself:

> Wait, Erica. It's fine to agree with your dad, but it sounds to me like you're doing so just because your dad hates him. Think for yourself. Look at the things Clinton *has* done: ban quite a few assault weapons from the streets, bring economic reform, get a good jobs bill passed, and at least give a good try at health care reform. I don't want to tell you to be a Democrat, but I just think you should think about things independently from your dad.

The fact that many of the messages that we studied had very quick response times strikes us as evidence that speedy responses matter to most students. As we said, the students are connected to the discourse and to each other ("involved," Deborah Tannen, 1989, and other linguists would say), and the possibility of turn-taking speed that mimics face-to-face conversation probably enhances the involvement.

Margaret Riel (1994) reminded us that involvement of this sort is what causes a particular technological innovation to be used in schools, rather than closeted. Technology itself, after all, does not change instructional practice of teachers or literacy behaviors of students. Teachers and students change by using new technology. Tony Scott, Michael Cole, and Martin Engel (1992) at the Laboratory of Comparative Human Cognition made a related point when they noted that some teachers just use computers as a machine to be understood (so they teach keyboarding and use of content-free software such as word processors and databases), some only use them as teacher substitutes (so, they focus on drill-and-practice programs), but some—the teachers whom we studied, for instance—use them as a tool to achieve powerful instructional goals.

The Office of Technology Assessment (OTA), until recently a research arm of the U.S. Congress, reported (OTA, 1995) that there are more than 2.8 million teachers at present in the United States. Most teachers have many years of teaching experience (the median is 15 years) and, at a median age of 42, most of them attended school before computers were used in classrooms. Some teachers are familiar with technology at home and eager to have it at school, whereas others are very unfamiliar and very anxious. Most teachers, the OTA report suggested, are probably somewhere between eager and anxious.

# INTERNET PROPONENTS AND OPPONENTS

If there is a contingent of scholars and others staking out a tentative middle ground on the issue of whether the Internet is going to change the way we teach and learn for better or worse, it must be small. Nearly everything that we have read, particularly in the popular press, has been written by someone whom we would characterize as proponent or opponent to widespread Internet use by children and adolescents.

Many proponents, such as New Zealand scholars John Tiffin and Lalita Rajasingham (1995, p. 120), have described a vision. Tiffin and Rajasingham's begins with each "telestudent" having a personal computing device, rather than pencils, exercise books, and texts. The computer links into a telecommunications system via modem and network account, so that the student can access databases, call up multimedia instructional programs, upload assignments, and then mail completed work back electronically, receiving individual assistance, as needed, from a distant instructor.

These activities are *asynchronous*, they occur in nonreal time, so the student can study during conventional school hours or in the middle of the night. And the student can work from home, work, or anywhere else where there is a telephone outlet. As Tiffin and Rajasingham (1995) noted enthusiastically, electronic libraries never close. (We should note that Tiffin and Rajasingham's vision extends well beyond this scenario. This is the starting place, and almost all of these pieces are in place already. In fact, we routinely use many of them, but not, however, the term *telestudent*.)

Nicholas Negroponte (1995), professor of media technology at the Massachusetts Institute of Technology (MIT) and founding director of the Media Lab, also has a vision of computers and Internet activity moving, in exponential fashion, into our daily lives. The data he provided are impressive: 30 million people estimated to be on the Internet now, the population increasing at 10% per month, the total number of Internet users—if this rate of growth were to continue (impossibly, of course)—exceeding the population of the world by 2003. The state of Maryland offers the Internet to all of its residents, Negroponte tells us, as does the city of Bologna, Italy. And the Internet is not North American anymore: The fastest growing number of Internet hosts in late 1994 were Argentina, Iran, Peru, Egypt, the Phillipines, the Russian Federation, Slovenia, and Indonesia, in that order.

Distance means little in the digital world. As Jill Ellsworth (1994) put it, "Australia is just as close as the state capital" (p. 6). In fact, a person often gets faster replies from more distant places than from ones close to home because the time change allows the receiver to respond while the sender sleeps.

Negroponte (1995) admits to being one of many "wimps on the net" (p. 182) because he uses the Internet strictly for e-mail, ignoring real-time discussion groups. He likes some of the same things about e-mail systems, about being asynchronous, that we like: It reduces the need for "telephone tag," which Negroponte defines as a game played to find the opportunity to be synchronous (often played for days, we would add). It is informal, as we said earlier. It is great for message-passing that requires no synchrony (e.g., distribution of office memos). It is not interruptive of one's thinking like a telephone. And, it supports rethinking, because messages can be processed at one's leisure, thoughtfully, and they can be edited (a really important point for novice correspondents in classrooms).

Like Batya Friedman (1991), Negroponte (1995) described telecommunications activity as intensely social. We particularly like this point about the Internet, the network of networks: "The true value of a network is less about information and more about community. The information superhighway is more than a short cut to every book in the Library of Congress. It is creating a totally new, global social fabric" (p. 183).

We agree that the educational value for Internet access lies in global community—in McLuhan's (1964) global village. And this makes us slightly less concerned about the places in *Technopoly*, in which Neil Postman (1993) argued that new technologies are altering society in disturbing ways, that information is dangerous when it has no place to go, when it has no higher purpose, and when there is no theory to which it applies. Negroponte's vision contextualizes classroom computer use in communication theory and pedagogy. It gives Internet activity in classrooms meaning and purpose beyond keyboarding, databases, and drill.

Proponents often celebrate the egalitarian nature of the Internet. Young and old, brainy and not-so-brainy, ugly and handsome persons can participate as long as they have the mechanical tools (computer, account, and telephone access), and each can decide how many personal characteristics to disclose to communication partners. The Internet is not nearly so hierarchical, so attentive to physical shortcomings and social status as, for instance, most high schools that we know.

This lack of cliquishness means that Internet participants can learn from and about persons with whom they would have little contact otherwise—perhaps a peer from Egypt or Peru, in any case, someone who might have a strikingly different world view and personal experiences. For instance, Negroponte tells the story about a high school student visiting him at MIT after "meeting" him (and Nobel Prize winners and senior executives) on the Internet.

Access to others is undeniably important to learning. Actually, access is also exactly what worries us about the Internet—unequal access, that is. As Scott et al. (1992) reminded us, there are inequalities in terms of gender, ethnicity, and class. Parents are more likely to buy computers for their sons than for their daughters. Ethnic-minority students in the United States must contend with the "Americanness" of keyboard layout, screen driver, menu structure, and icon design whenever they use computers.

And, perhaps most disturbing of all, computers and telephone access seem very much a luxury to poor families and poor school districts who regularly grapple with putting nutritious food on the table and certified teachers in the classrooms. Reported in an *New York Times* (1995) editorial was Department of Commerce data revealing that about 20% of the poorest households in the United States do not have telephones and will surely not be able to purchase computers and related equipment. They will be "information have-nots."

It is asserted in the *Times* editorial that public libraries—which have been overrun with requests for Internet searches for students and job information for their parents in households without access—need some sort of telephone rate relief. Right now, libraries in New York have had to limit services because of data transmission costs over *local loops* (the dedicated lines between local libraries and the central libraries that have sophisticated computer-searching capabilities). If the New York Public Service Commission does not mandate reduced data-transmission rates over local loops for libraries, middle-class and wealthy children in New York will be part of the information age, and poor children will not—an intolerable situation in a democratic society that espouses the principle of an informed citizenry. Needless to say, New York is not alone; most other states face the same issue of inequity of access linked to economic status.

Also, in a very recent report Sheila Heaviside, Elizabeth Farris, Gerald Malitz, and Judi Carpenter (1995) reported from the National Center for Education Statistics (NCES) we are told that even though 75% percent of public schools have computers with some type of telecommunications capability, only 35% have access to the Internet. More secondary schools have access than elementary schools, and larger schools (with enrollments of 1,000 or more) are about twice as likely as small schools (with enrollments of less than 300) to have access. A disturbing statistic is that only 3% of all instructional rooms (classrooms, labs, media centers) are connected to the Internet. The overwhelming number of elementary and secondary school connections are available to building administrators for record-keeping, not to teachers and students for communication.

It was made clear in the NCES report that funding is the major barrier to teacher and student Internet access. Henry Becker's (1995) survey data give us funding detail: It generally costs about $86,000 to do electrical work and classroom remodeling necessary to establish the local area network, there are additional one-time costs for Internet connectivity, and there are recurring costs of about $9,000 each year in access fees. Poor districts have tremendous difficulty in securing this level of funding without benefactor involvement. This is because schools are funded almost exclusively by a combination of state and local taxpayers. In fact, in what Jonathan Kozol (1991) called "the arcane machinery by which we finance public education" (p. 54), the local property tax is the decisive force in shaping inequality of resources.

Because the property tax depends on the taxable value of local homes and industries, a wealthy suburb in which homes are worth upwards of $400,000 draws on a larger tax base in proportion to its student population than a city occupied by thousands of poor people. Even if city residents tax themselves at several times the rate of a very wealthy suburban district, they are likely to have less money to spend per child in their schools. If the federal government and private businesses do not support computer purchases and Internet access (in principle and with dollars), the nation's public schools will continue to buy computers, printers, and communications devices—in the *Times*, Laurie Flynn (1995) reported overall expenditures in 1994–1995 of roughly $2.5 billion—but some schools will have them, and others will not.

There is another sort of access issue that concerns us as well. In this instance, student access is not hindered by pervasive social and economic factors like sexism, ethnocentrism, or poverty, but by the conservative ideology of vocal network opponents who are certain that the Internet allows children and adolescents to experience pornography on a regular basis.

Nebraska Senator James Exon says that pornographic pictures can be downloaded from the Internet and displayed on a home computer—old news for computer-savvy undergraduates, reported Philip Elmer-Dewitt in a *Time* magazine (1995) cover story report on Exon. The 1995 Exon-Coats revision of the Communications Decency Act, in which it was proposed to outlaw obscene material and impose fines of up to $100,000 and prison terms on anyone who knowingly makes "indecent" material available on a computer network to children under 18, was widely attacked as an assault on the First Amendment, but it passed 84 to 16 in the Senate. (Perhaps of secondary importance, it was quickly pronounced to be unworkable. It is almost impossible to control a decentralized network of more than 50,000 separate networks.) Negroponte (1995) reminded us that the Internet is a massive global network of networks, with no designer in charge, keeping its shape like a formation of ducks of equal status, with no boss whatsoever.)

The key issue, according to *Time*'s unnamed legal scholars, is whether the Internet is a print medium (like a newspaper), which enjoys protection against government interference, or a broadcast medium (like television), which is subject to all sorts of government control. During the summer of 1995 debate on the wisdom of Exon-Coats, odd bedfellows emerged: House Speaker Newt Gingrich joined civil libertarians and House representatives from both political parties in denouncing violation of free speech provisions and in searching for ways to help parents, not the government, decide how to "lock out" their children's access to material they find objectionable.

This whole discussion—replete with powerful men waving "raw" images about on the Senate floor (and thus on C-Span)–really addresses sexually explicit images on bulletin-board systems (BBSs), for which proof of age is required, not e-mail between classrooms. Bulletin boards—which Howard Rheingold (1994) described as "unedited, often unpolished, sometimes offensive to traditional sensibilities" (p. 132),—are very topic focused, and sex is only one of many topics. In the San Francisco Bay Area, for instance, one can read about alternative health issues on The Grateful

Med BBS, about earthquakes on the Public Seismic Network, about mostly straight sex on Kinky Komputer, and about issues of interest to veterans, Zionists, White supremacists, environmentalists, feminists, libertarians, animal rights activists, Asian-Americans (and many more groups) on one BBS or another.

Senators and others who confuse adult BBS activity with children's classroom Internet communication—and who do so in a public forum—have an impact: An international medium is potentially restricted by U.S. legislation. And, parents everywhere worry. In Michigan, for instance, we attended a school meeting last spring in which a group of parents mentioned pornography (and potential adult "stalking" of youngsters by way of e-mail addresses) and then balked at spending tax dollars to provide Internet access for their school.

# TO SUM UP

In this book, we tell stories about classrooms. Each story is, at least in part, about why and how a teacher and students in one classroom communicate with teachers and students in other classrooms. In each case, we present their *very words,* sent over the Internet far more quickly than we can write this summary. Each classroom is a context, as is the Internet itself. We try to understand Internet discourse, something that we know is quite different from most classroom discourse, something that is certainly not typical written language but not quite oral language either.

We have some knowledge, of course, about what Nicholas Negroponte (1995) told us happens when teachers and students send messages over the Internet—how the messages are decomposed into packets and given headers with an address, then are sent over various paths through intermediate processors that strip off and add other information, and finally are reordered and assembled at the other end—but we mostly care about the intensely social activity that occurs, about how teachers and students connect with other teachers and students who, in many cases, are hundreds, even thousands, of miles away. It is because of the enormous potential for communication beyond the bounds of one's own classroom, one's local community, that we tell these stories. Our first story is about Ruth Coleman's fifth-grade classroom in Joliet, IL.

# II

## Internet Communication in Six Classrooms

# 2

# Ruth Coleman's Fifth-Grade Classroom: Involvement Strategies

When those of us who do not live there think about Illinois, we usually think of Chicago, a city of about 3 million people and a raucous past that includes a Great Fire, Prohibition-era massacres, big-time blues, and National Basketball Association titles. We do not, typically, think of Joliet, a city of only about 80,000.

Joliet sits on the edge of the prairie, about 40 miles southwest of Chicago. Looking in all directions except northeast, one sees fields of corn and soybean for miles. Colleges and malls are there, as everywhere, but in this part of the country, they are scatterings of buildings in the middle of large fields. If Joliet is dwarfed by Chicago, it, in turn, dwarfs hundreds of small towns nearby. Illinois is mostly small towns, some with such peculiar names that Lorrie Moore (1990) could tell us about a headline that read, "Normal Man Marries Oblong Woman" (p. 67).

The Des Plaines River flows right through the middle of Joliet, and there is heavy boat and barge traffic moving grain toward the Mississippi. An improbable newcomer to the river is a fleet of gambling boats; the boats, with glamorous names such as the *Empress River Casino* and *Harrah's Northern Star,* advertise their existence on giant billboards in and around Chicago. Revenue from the boats flows to the city of Joliet for street improvements and downtown renewal.

America's first public community college is in Joliet. So is the state prison and Caterpillar Tractor Company, manufacturer of heavy equipment, some of it used locally and some shipped overseas.

Thomas Jefferson School is on the west side of town. The building is brick, 25 years old, just new enough to have air conditioning for warm spring and fall days. It is not a magnet or selective school, the sort of school that Jonathan Kozol (1991) described as essentially a private school operated within a public school system. It is a neighborhood school. Many of the children who attend Jefferson trudge off to school on foot, but other means of transportation exist: Some children, participants in a school desegregation plan, arrive by bus from as far away as 5 miles. Another group of children also come on the bus because a school that was about 2 miles from Jefferson closed its doors recently. Jefferson houses kindergarten through fifth-grade classes and some additional classes for children with a variety of special needs.

## LIFE IN RUTH COLEMAN'S FIFTH-GRADE CLASSROOM

Philip Jackson (1990), writing about the predictability of classrooms, noted that no one entering one is likely to mistake it for a living room, grocery store, or train station. He noted, however, that elementary school teachers usually spend considerable time fussing with their rooms' decoration.

Ruth Coleman's fifth-grade room at Jefferson is no exception. This past year, they had a "pet" cocoon that one of the children brought in during the fall, hoping that a butterfly or moth would emerge come spring, and they had two Apple IIe computers and two printers (but not a modem, which was available only in the computer lab in the school library). A vestigial "decoration" is a red light in the room that flashes warnings of a fire or tornado; this room, which is now home to Ruth Coleman's fifth grade, used to house hearing-impaired students, and they could not, of course, hear an alarm, so the light was installed some years back.

Classroom events in Ruth Coleman's room are, as in every class, a mix of the predictable and the unpredictable. Events that occur with some regularity are the following: Each week, a Student of the Week is selected, and the person receives a certificate and pencil and then serves as Ruth Coleman's special helper that week. The school day is divided fairly predictably into periods during which specific subjects are studied and certain activities are sanctioned; during silent reading, for instance, students are allowed to sit in the book corner to read books that they select from the classroom library.

During a long language arts period (9:00 a.m. to 11:15 a.m. each morning), writing takes place, some of it writing to other students on the Internet. Because there is no Internet connection in the classroom, this is a fairly complicated process: Children compose on paper or at one of the two computers whenever they have time (i.e., when they are finished with assigned work). They use the printers to share messages with each other and to edit each other's work. Finished correspondence is saved on a floppy disk that Ruth takes home. There she uses America Online, which provides Internet access, to send batches of messages.

Children leave the classroom at various times during the day. Their most frequent destination as a group is probably the aptly named "all-purpose room," which serves as gymnasium, lunch room, and gathering place for all school-wide assemblies. Other students leave the room individually or in small groups: Five have been identified as "gifted," and they leave once a week for something called PLUS. Some children participate in band or orchestra. Some leave to serve as crossing guards. A few students have been selected as computer tutors, and they leave to work with first graders. Ruth Coleman described this traffic pattern and then added, "It sounds like we never get anything done—except leave the room!"

School reformers like Deborah Meier (Mosle, 1995a) are proponents of what has been called a 20–20 vision (i.e., no more than 20 students per classroom, no more than 20 teachers in a school, thus no school populated by more than 400 students). Reformers cite recent research that demonstrates that a school's size is even more important in determining students' performance on nationwide tests than the amount spent per pupil. Ruth Coleman's classroom this past year was a little crowded by this maxim (26 students, half of whom were girls), but the school size of 380 is appealing.

Ruth came to the profession late. She raised four sons and then returned to college to prepare for a career in teaching. Outside the classroom, she has been surrounded by males, all immersed in technology: husband, Jack, a systems analyst for 36 years at Caterpillar, and her sons who early on established a small business in their home printing mailing labels for local Joliet organizations, one going on to become a computer scientist at Argonne National Laboratory. Inside the classroom, she became involved in, among other things, the AT&T "Learning Circles" project designed by Margaret Riel (1994). Learning Circles was designed to use the Internet to connect classrooms across considerable distance in the exploration of themes such as community history and environmental issues. This past year, Ruth corresponded with a group of students from the University of Wisconsin. They wanted to interview her about how she got interested in students' writing on the Internet and how she integrated this writing with other parts of her curriculum.

Ruth says she believes that communication with persons at a distance by way of the Internet supports new forms of community. Teachers can communicate with other teachers, students with other students, all acquiring new knowledge and skills as a result. However, as Margaret Riel (1994) pointed out, the social skills needed to make this rapid communication work must be learned. Some of what occurred as children in Ruth Coleman's class wrote to children living in a small village in Alaska was learning some of these new social skills. (In this chapter, we focus on Joliet and learning about new ways to use language. In the next chapter, we take a closer look at the Alaskan village and at learning about a different culture.)

## LEARNING NEW WAYS TO USE LANGUAGE: INVOLVEMENT ON THE INTERNET

Ruth Coleman says she thinks that the children in her classroom this past year learned a great deal about what linguists call "involvement." When one person converses with another, involvement can occur. Directly through words or indirectly through nonverbal communication (e.g., gesture), speaker and listener can respond to each other: You tell me that your mother is ill; I frown, I move toward you, and I tell you about my recent experience with a seriously ill parent. We are involved, we are participating in a conversation. Involvement is more than understanding. (Think of a person who, on hearing from you that your mother is ill, stands impassive and mute. The person might be able to relate the details of your mother's condition to a third person—evidence of understanding—but, without any verbal or nonverbal connection to you, there is not involvement.)

Deborah Tannen (1989) and others noted that involvement occurs more readily within, rather than across, cultures. This is easy to understand because differences in background knowledge and in conversational style (part of our cultural identities) can lead to misunderstandings and misjudgments about another person's intentions. Even when regional and ethnic group are similar, there is great potential for conversational crosspurposes across genders. Deborah Tannen's (1990) book *You Just Don't Understand* documents that a mostly male preference for using conversation to maintain the upper hand and a mostly female preference to use conversation to seek confirmation and to reach consensus can lead to difficulty when men and women converse with each other.

How do we achieve some level of involvement when we cannot rely on gesture or other nonverbal means and must use words alone? That is, how do we work on involvement when our conversational partners are many miles away, connected only by the Internet?

## Repetition

Tad, a student in Ruth Coleman's class, did something intriguing. On a warm September day, just after the start of school, he was obviously interested in the weather, and was also interested, it seems, in what the children in Alaska would have to say about it. He wrote:

> . . . It is around 80 degrees here in the daytime now. How about there? Is there snow always up there? We wear shorts and T-shirts to school now. Later, it will get chilly as Fall comes, and Winter. Then we will wear warmer clothes. What do you wear? Soon the trees will turn beautiful bright colors. Then the leaves fall off. . . .

Not long after, four girls in Alaska wrote back:

> . . . I am slways using jackets to school and clothes. . . . (Elizabeth A.)

> . . . In winter I wear snow pants. . . . (Elizabeth K.)

> . . . 55 degrees today. . . . (Stacy)

> . . . I have a Parka, but it is used in winter time. . . . (Grace)

Tad and the four girls engaged in an involvement strategy that Deborah Tannen (1989) and others would call "repetition." The girls did not repeat Tad's exact words, but they picked up on his topic and transformed his questions into their statements. Whether Tad and the girls knowingly or unknowingly achieved involvement in this way is unclear. In either case, Tad was quite good at being involved. Between early September and early October, 56 questions were posed by children in Joliet or Alaska, and Tad posed 10 of them. Many of his questions prompted statements a day or so later from Alaska.

Some repetition takes place over many messages. During the early fall, Grace in Alaska mentioned "rock people" in one of her messages:

> . . . We have rock people. I speak Yupik. IF you want to climb up to the rock people you will have to wear you rubber boots. Yesterday I went up to the rock people. . . .

A few days later, Doris sent a note from Joliet, asking directly about rock people and providing a guess about what they might be:

I want to know what you mean when you say "rock people". What are they? We guessed that they are rocks that look like people. Can you climb on them? On our playground we have old tires to climb up on, besides lots of jungle gyms, and bars to climb on. We have a slide, swings, and a merry go round, too. . . .

A few days after that, Jadine in Joliet weighed in with a repetition of the question from Doris, adding some emphasis of her own:

. . . We still do not understand what are your "rock people?" Please explain more about them. We are dying to figure this out! . . .

And, not too many days later, three separate messages came from Alaska, resolving, more or less, the issue of what rock people are:

The rock people are just a stack of rocks, big rocks. . . . (Jeffrey)

The rock people are just a pile of rocks, flat rocks. If you go up you will see the whole village and the pond and ocean. And you will be scared. At the rock people it is cool. If you go down to the village after you were cold, and if you go down it will be hot. (Grace)

The rock people are just stacks of rocks. There is about tem rock rock people. . . . (Tommy)

This is involvement. Grace, Doris, Jadine, Jeffrey, and Tommy participated in a long-distance conversation, using words alone to connect with each other. Statements were transformed into questions, questions into statements. The children were connected to the Internet exchange and to each other, despite considerable distance between classrooms.

A really interesting sort of repetition—and obvious involvement—occurred between two pairs of girls in the two classrooms. Even though Ruth Coleman treated all correspondence as communal, reading notes aloud to the class and then posting them for rereading, these girls linked up early in the exchanges between classrooms and continued to write almost exclusively to each other for the entire school year.

Betsey in Joliet and Elizabeth A. in Alaska were one of the pairs. The repetition in some of their messages is quite stunning. In an exchange about themselves from mid-September, the girls repeated topics, and they repeated them in exactly the same order:

My name is Betsey. I am a girl. I go to Thomas Jefferson School. I live close to school, so I walk. I am very interested in Alaskan culture. . . .

Hi I am Elizabeth. I am a girl. I go to (P.T.A.M.s) Paul T. albert Memorial School. I live almost by the school but not to close to it. I walk too. We are Eskimo culture. . . .

When experts advise novice writers about what to write about, they often suggest the details of one's own life as a starting place. Anne Lamott (1994) is not alone in advising that inexperienced writers should write down all the things that you swore you'd never tell another soul. After all, she reminded us, we own what happened to us.

However, in Ruth Coleman's class, only the girls formed exclusive-pair relationships and then divulged personal details to their correspondents. Perhaps this is not very surprising. While we are growing up, we establish patterns of using language, and little girls' friendships are often made and maintained by telling secrets. As a matter of fact, the pattern of females' talking about what happened during a day, how one felt when it happened, does not wholly disappear in adulthood.

Jadine, a Black girl who is new to Jefferson this year, is a child whom Ruth Coleman frets about because, despite being academically successful, she is a social isolate, with neither Black nor White friends. Jadine is the Joliet member of the second pair of mostly exclusive correspondents. She writes often to Stacy, telling her important secrets about herself:

Dear Stacy, It's me, Jadine. I forgot to tell you I have three sisters. One is 7, the other is 4. My younger sister is 11 months. My grandmother accuses me of everything. I had my baby sister on my shoulder and my grandmother told my cousin to take my sister away from me. DO you have any sisters or brothers? One day my grandmother said I stole two dollars. Before I came to Thomas Jefferson I went to HOLY FAMILY. It is a Catholic School. We went to mass every Friday. Mass is like church but in mass you stand, sit, and kneel. It was ok, if you were flexible. I like Jefferson better. Did you ever change schools. if you did, which did you like better? I have to go! Bye! Jadine

So, it seems that repetition was used by Tad and the four girls who were interested in the weather, all of the children who wrote back and forth about the rock people, and the pairs of girls who established mostly exclusive writing relationships, possibly with some amount of intent to achieve involvement (of course we cannot be wholly certain about the children's intentions). The result of all this repetition was that participants in the exchanges were linked to the discourse and to each other.

Leaving the pairs of girls aside temporarily, it is interesting to note that Tad's writing about the weather and Grace's mentioning the rock people were influential (i.e., other children responded to them), whereas other writing was not. That is, some messages triggered other messages, whereas other messages had little apparent impact.

We think that the best explanation for influence of this sort is topic interest—what Ulrich Schiefele (1992) described as a relatively enduring preference for particular topics, subject areas, or activities. We all have some preferences, but not about the same topics. I like to read mysteries, whereas you prefer historical fiction, and I like to discuss politics, whereas you prefer talking about your organic gardening. When given the opportunity to write about and in response to a range of topics, children in Ruth Coleman's class picked topics that John Dewey (1900) would describe as having inherent attracting power—interest—for them. The topics initiated by Tad and Grace were apparently of broad interest.

## Detail

Consider again part of Jadine's note to Stacy—this time, not for its secrets, but for the considerable detail that Jadine provides:

> . . . I forgot to tell you I have three sisters. One is 7, the other is 4. My younger sister is 11 months. My grandmother accuses me of everything. I had my baby sister on my shoulder and my grandmother told my cousin to take my sister away from me. DO you have any sisters or brothers? One day my grandmother said I stole two dollars. Before I came to Thomas Jefferson I went to HOLY FAMILY. It is a Catholic School. We went to mass every Friday. Mass is like church but in mass you stand, sit, and kneel. It was ok, if you were flexible. I like Jefferson better. . . .

She might have written only that she had three sisters, but instead she wrote the ages of each. She might have said simply that she was sometimes treated unfairly, but instead she wrote in some detail about her grandmother's accusation. She might have noted that she used to go to a Catholic school and left it at that; instead she named the school and described the Mass. (An aside: Neither Ruth Coleman nor we can sort out whether Jadine intends "flexible" to refer to standing, sitting, and kneeling during the Mass or to acceptance of the tenets of the Church.)

Jadine was not the only student in Ruth's class who provided rich detail. Note that both Seth and Ondine wrote at least four topic-linked sentences, rich in detail on family and a broken arm, respectively:

> . . . My sister goes to college in India. She wants to be a doctor. My family is from India. My Grandma still lives there. . . . (Seth)

... I have a little brother, who broke his arm last week. I never broke any bones, have you? Do you have a doctor in your village, or a hospital? What happens if you get sick or break a bone? We go to our doctor's office, or to the emergency room at the hospital. . . . (Ondine)

Deborah Tannen (1989) suggested that detail can make an idea particular, familiar, and memorable. Details set a scene and provide a sense of authenticity by naming recognizable people (e.g., a grandmother, a little brother, a doctor); places (Catholic school, India, the emergency room); and activities (Mass, setting of a broken bone).

## Sense of Audience, Rhetorical Choices

Of course, the children in Ruth Coleman's class were corresponding with children some distance away—geographically and culturally. Some of the people, places, and activities that they mentioned might not be recognizable to the children in Alaska. To both Jadine's and Ondine's credit, they seem aware that their audiences may not know what they know about Mass or emergency rooms (thus, the definitional "Mass is like church but..." and the query, "Do you have a doctor in your village, or a hospital?"). When speakers or writers show this sense of audience and also provide plenty of detail, listeners and readers are able to generate mental images of unfamiliar objects and events. This is surely what occurred in the rock people exchange, when the children in Alaska described the rock people to the children in Ruth Coleman's class, who had never seen them.

Sense of audience is an important element in using words alone to achieve involvement. It is tricky for relatively young writers in that they are negotiating new territory. In Ruth Coleman's classroom—as in most classrooms—much of the speaking and writing is to and for the teacher, not fellow students. In the Internet communication, other children receive and respond to communication. So, different rhetorical choices must be made, less along the lines of "What does she want to hear?" and more along the lines of "What is he likely to know about *X?* How much background information should I provide?"

Gordon Wells and Gen Ling Chang-Wells (1992) are interested in children's negotiation of this new rhetorical territory, just as we are. They suggested that the situation of children communicating with peers (face-to-face or not) allows them to discover the limitations of their own knowledge and of the way in which they have presented it to their audiences.

Questioning by one's audience is one clear index to communication failure. Note a segment of the rock people exchange in this regard:

> . . . We have rock people. I speak Yupik. IF you want to climb up to the rock people you will have to wear you rubber boots. Yesterday I went up to the rock people. . . . (Grace, in Alaska)

> I want to know what you mean when you say "rock people". What are they? We guessed that they are rocks that look like people. Can you climb on them? . . . (Doris, in Joliet)

Grace could only conclude that, even though she knows what the rock people are, Doris and other students in Ruth Coleman's classroom do not. Her response to their confusion is a wise one—elaboration, a more detailed description of the rock people:

> The rock people are just a pile of rocks, flat rocks. If you go up you will see the whole village and the pond and ocean. And you will be scared. At the rock people it is cool. If you go down to the village after you were cold, and if you go down it will be hot.

Grace's audience (and Doris' too) is, for the most part, unknown. The children in Joliet and the children in Alaska have not met. They have exchanged a number of messages over the course of the school year, but there are many aspects of each others' lives about which they know very little. Until the classes decided to exchange videotapes during the winter, the students could only imagine what each other looked and sounded like. A writer, any writer, imagines an audience, and the children in Ruth Coleman's class and their correspondents in Alaska are no different from other writers in this regard. They have to guess at what their correspondents know, and they have to reformulate what they have to say after they guess incorrectly and are told as much by their readers at the other end of the communication.

This imagining and guessing is part of what developmental psychologists call "perspective-taking." As Patricia Miller noted (1983), younger children than those in Ruth Coleman's class are not very adept at taking another person's perceptual or conceptual perspective. She gives the example of a child's holding a book upright, pointing to a picture, and asking his mother, "What's this?" In this case, the child does not recognize that his mother, who is facing him, can only see the back of the book and has no idea what appears on the page.

Because young children cannot easily take other persons' perspectives, they make little effort to tailor their language to meet the needs of listeners or readers. They may leave important events out of narratives and refer to "her" and "it," without making clear to whom and to what they are referring.

The children in Ruth Coleman's class are more adept than this; they experience some difficulties with role-taking and communication (as do students all the way through college), but the children are able to adjust and reformulate their messages after being made aware of the need.

And, an interesting note: Peers may be excellent sources of prompts to reformulate. Unlike adults (especially parents), who take the child into account so efficiently that they impede reformulation (e.g., moving around the child to look at the picture, without commenting on the need to do so), peers are willing to be critical. Perhaps if adults behaved differently, children would develop competence in communication more quickly. As John Flavell, Patricia Miller, and Scott Miller (1993) noted, in school, children encounter frequent and explicit demands to communicate clearly.

## Revision When Writing Is Practiced As a Social Activity

Writing instruction sometimes leads children to believe that writing is a bundle of cognitive skills, rather than a highly interactive, social activity, in which someone composes text in order to communicate ideas to someone else, all the while making rhetorical decisions of the sort that we have been discussing—repeating to connect, adding detail to clarify, and so on. Most classroom writing tasks seem better framed as exercises in teacher evaluation of skill than as practice in learning to communicate. Think about Arthur Applebee's (1991) description of the typical high school writing assignment: first and final drafts on a prescribed topic, a page or less in length, graded by the teacher.

Writing on the Internet provides an audience beyond the teacher (one that writes back about ideas, not stylistic flaws!), and it allows for choice of topic and length of message. Surely Ruth Coleman did not assign "a short message on the topic of the weather" to Tad and "a slightly longer message about accusations" to Jadine. In Internet writing, the children write about what they know about and are interested in. Instead of isolated assignments, messages are linked to each other (an excellent example is the series of messages about the rock people).

When classroom writing on the Internet is seen as communication, not as a bundle of skills, revision of first efforts involves deciding whether something needs to be defined, connected, elaborated, eliminated, rather than merely spelled or punctuated differently. Message senders take message receivers' perspectives, as much as possible. As Martin Nystrand (1989) described it, they monitor how well the message is going on the basis of whether there are likely to be trouble spots for their readers. Trouble spots can include such unconventional spelling or confusing punctuation that text is likely to be incomprehensible to even a forgiving reader, but it is a great deal more than that.

Notice how one student in Ruth Coleman's class, Edward, reworked a November message before sending it off to Alaska. Here is the first draft, composed on paper:

> Guess what? We had a fire in our neighborhood. It started when my friend and I were going to my house. When we saw a fire starting in my neiboors garage. We raced over and told them. Then I raced to tell my mom. She dialed 911. The fire Department was able to put out the fire. Then we were invited to city hall to get an award for bravery from the mayor.

Here is the revised copy, fixed by Edward at the computer and sent off to Alaska:

> Guess what? We had a fire in our neighborhood. It all started when my friend and I were going to my house and we noticed a fire in my neighbor's garage. We raced to their house and notified them that their garage was on fire. Then I raced home to tell my parents. My mom dialed 911. The fire department was able to put the fire out. A few days later, we were invited to City Hall to get an award for bravery from our mayor, Mayor Schultz.

Important changes were made, perhaps, in part, a result of peer editing, which occurs frequently in Ruth Coleman's classroom. First, there are the obvious mechanical fix-ups—in spelling ("neighbor's"), punctuation (removal of the fragment "When we saw . . . "), and capitalization ("City Hall"). But there is more. There is less ambiguity in the second version ("We raced over and told them" becomes "We raced to their house and notified them that their garage was on fire."). There is a little more detail ("our mayor, Mayor Schultz"). We have the sense in reading both versions that Edward monitored trouble spots for his readers in Alaska and revised the message accordingly.

Tad, the student with the interest in weather, did something similar with a November message. His first draft, again composed on paper, appeared as follows:

> On Halloween we had a party in our room. We had lots of candy. We also played Bingo. Some of the kinds of candy we got were a rice crispie treat, a little skeleton skull with treats in it, and some small Snickers. We also had neat costumes in our class. It was a fun party!

In the revised copy, ready to be sent to Alaska, the important revision was structural:

> On Halloween we had a party in our room. We were given lots of treats. Some of the treats were rice crispies, a little skeleton skull with little treats inside, and some little Snickers. We also played about 15–20 rounds of bingo. We also had some neat costumes in our class. It was a fun party.

Gone are the jerky topic shifts of the first draft (a result of Tad's telling what he knows, with little attention to order of telling); readers will not need to "shift gears" from candy to bingo to candy to skeleton skulls and back to candy. Instead, a general statement is provided ("We were given lots of treats"). This statement is superordinate to the list of treats that follows. Bingo is discussed after the treats—and in a little more detail. Overall, local coherence is considerably improved; a significant trouble spot for readers has been fixed.

Linda is another student in Ruth Coleman's class who revised her draft message that she had composed on paper when she moved to the computer. The handwritten message read as follows:

> Well a cople of days ago the band and orcestra went on a trip. we went to go to see the chicago symphony. first we went on a 2 hour drive to chicago then every band and orcestra student and some parents whent to Mcdonalds we ate there. My mom was incharge of a couple of students. I dont think she new that i spit on somebodys food down on the first flor. Then we went to the orchistra hall where they were playing and we listen to Boring music i only new about 5 songs then we went home and I guess thats it By.

In the revised copy, there are many improvements:

> Well, a couple of days ago the Band and Orchestra went on a trip. We went to go to see the Chicago symphony. First we went on a 2 hour drive to Chicago. Then every band and every orchestra student, and some parents went to MacDonalds, where we ate. My mom was in charge of a couple of students. I don't think she knew that I spit on somebody's food down on the first floor. Then we went to the Orchestra Hall where they were playing, and we listened to boring music. I only knew about 5 songs. Then we went home and I guess that's it. Bye.

There are many corrections in spelling ("couple," "orchestra," "knew," "floor," "listened") and capitalization (first words in sentences, "Chicago," "I," "boring"), and run-on sentences, contractions, and possessives are fixed.

However, we include Linda's message in both versions to illustrate some things that were not changed. Ruth Coleman did not impose a more formal, less conversational style on Linda, who begins both versions with "Well . . . " and ends both with " . . . and I guess that's it," and she also did not nudge Linda to remove either the spitting anecdote or the description of the music as boring. In other words, reducing trouble spots for readers does not mean tampering with the individual style or content preferences of the writer; it means reworking a communication to make the job of the reader easier.

Application of reader-sensitive remedies requires an "aha" by either writers or their peer editors that something is wrong, that a trouble spot exists. Adeptness at monitoring one's comprehension and composition success is age-related, but as we pointed out elsewhere (Garner, 1987), it is also influenced by instruction. When teachers like Ruth Coleman ask young writers to revise their drafts—and to seek assistance from peers who are less wedded to word and phrase than they—monitoring gradually becomes a routine, student-initiated activity.

At the beginning of the year, Ruth Coleman provided considerable support for the revising process: She modeled how to monitor and apply remedies by putting writing samples on the overhead projector and asking the class to work together to find and reduce trouble spots for readers. By year's end, this was much less necessary. The children composed at the computer, often in pairs, editing as they wrote. Occasionally, they would still print out a draft, read it for trouble spots, and then get back on the computer to revise before saving and mailing.

The very fact that the children in Ruth Coleman's class can choose topic, length, and audience for much of what they write means that they are likely to care about their written work, to be willing to expend a little extra energy to fix it up if it is not, in their view, ready for a distant audience.

Jill Ellsworth (1994) told us that young writers want to be understood by their readers and that they are willing to work at improving comprehensibility of their messages. And Moshe Cohen and Margaret Riel (1989) found that when seventh-grade students wrote two compositions, one required as a midterm examination and the other addressed to peers in other countries and transmitted electronically, teachers scored the papers written for peers as significantly better in content, organization, and language use. One difference noted by the teacher–raters is exactly what we have been discussing: Writers had enough sense of audience to know that their readers some distance away might not share their background knowledge. They eliminated this potential trouble spot by being more explicit, by including more detail.

# WHAT WAS LEARNED IN RUTH COLEMAN'S CLASS THIS YEAR?

Many of the children learned how to use language in ways that promoted involvement. They learned that repeating topics, sometimes in exactly the same order, connects you to your audience. They learned how to use detail to make ideas particular, familiar, and memorable. Some of them acquired a strong sense of audience and came to realize that they needed to reformulate what they had written, tailoring their language to meet the needs of their readers many miles away. Nearly all of them learned how to monitor their written communication for trouble spots, such as unconventional spelling and punctuation, absence of local coherence, and ambiguity. They learned all of this, Ruth Coleman says she believes, because they participated in a year-long cycle of sending messages, receiving responses, and sending some more messages. They wrote to other children, and they wrote about topics of interest to them and their readers.

Certainly the children also learned that Internet communication can be fun. We conclude this, in part, from their own words, pieces of messages sent early in the year:

> . . . Well, I hope you write back. (Tad)

> . . . I can't wait til you write back. (Edward)

> . . . Please write back. (Seth)

> . . . I am looking forward to your next letter. We will read them to the whole class. We also put them up on the wall, so everyone can read them over and over. (Betsey)

> . . . We have two 5th grade classes. The other classes are not writing. I am glad we get to. (Kendra)

We also conclude that the activity was fun from a series of messages that Betsey sent to us. Betsey, a gifted writer who learned very early in the year how to compose at the computer, became our informant (along with Ruth Coleman) on how Internet communication was progressing in the classroom. In an especially touching message written just as the school year was ending in June, she wrote:

I'm sorry I haven't written in a long time. I have been so busy the past month I almost completely forgot about you. Well, I don't think I will be writing back, with school ending and all. Also today, in the middle of the night we will be leaving for Texas. In the end of the summer, we will be moving there. I can't wait. My dad might buy a gas station down there. My mom said she will buy me a horse just like the one at the old stable and board it at the nearest barn. We just bought a motor home or an RV, whatever you want to call it, so we won't be cramped in the van with all the stuff. My dad just bought a tv with a built in vcr so we won't be board in the RV. It is so cool. It is like a little home on wheels. Remember when I told you my dad got his arm crushed while working, well that is one of the reasons why we are moving. You see, when it gets cold my dad's arm starts to throb in pain and he can't take it no more, so we are going to live nere my grandma. I wish you could write back and tell me what's new but I din't remember my Prodigy number. When I find it I will write to Mrs. Coleman and she will give it to you.

What did Ruth learn? It is often said about a variety of innovations and reforms (computers and Internet communication among them) that they seldom affect teachers and their teaching in any meaningful way. As Virginia Richardson (1990) put it, many scholars believe that school organization and teacher beliefs and attitudes conspire to prevent broad implementation of reforms aimed at classrooms. Or, as David Cohen (1988) noted, innovations sweep across the nation's schools, find thousands of adoptions, but then disappear quickly, leaving few traces of their existence.

What Cohen (1988) and Richardson (1990) go on to say is very important. Cohen argued that if we look for significant instructional innovation in parts of the educational establishment rather than looking for it on average we will find more of it. Richardson noted that teaching is a highly personal sort of activity, that some teachers do change their own practice—in fact, some do it all the time, usually for reasons that they can articulate quite clearly.

Ruth Coleman strikes us as one of these teachers. We know that she tried new activities (e.g., Learning Circles, the Joliet–Alaska communication), that she shifted emphases (e.g., from mostly teacher editing of students' writing to considerable peer editing), and that she learned some new procedures along with the children (e.g., techniques for reformulating messages when distant readers are confused). She told us on many occasions that she was excited about the enthusiasm that the children exhibited, the fun they were having, while corresponding with the children in Alaska. In fact, this seems to be the single most important reason for Ruth Coleman's desire to incorporate Internet communication in her classroom.

She did not adopt an entirely new teaching philosophy. In a series of messages written to teachers in Alaska just before the school year began, she outlined some of her plans about what she would teach and how she would teach it (e.g., reading a single novel as a class, one chapter per day; starting the school year with some basic rules for polite and thoughtful conduct; using library resources to augment classroom texts), and her plans would not be characterized by most of us as radical. There were intentions to have plenty of activity and conversation, but there were also expectations that students would sometimes sit quietly in their seats and practice instructed skills, master specified content, and be nominated to speak in whole-class discussions. In other words, Ruth Coleman is not a teacher who discarded all of her old information sources and instructional tools once she discovered the Internet; neither, however, is she unwilling to experiment.

Ruth was rewarded this year for her experimentation. During the fall, she applied for an Ameritech/Golden Apple Foundation teacher's grant. In early February, she was notified that she would receive $5,000 in grant money so that for next year, she can purchase a modem, a phone line in her classroom, and a new computer—all of this coming at a time when computer equipment and on-line service are getting cheaper, faster, and more powerful. This means, of course, that she no longer has to resort to sending messages from home: Internet access is now available within her classroom. The district celebrated Ruth's success with an article in the June issue of the newsletter, *A Class Act,* sent to teachers in three neighboring counties.

Next year in Ruth Coleman's classroom, a new Internet writing project will be launched—not because it is mandated by the district, but because Ruth believes that this year's went so well. The project may involve classroom-to-classroom writing or something else entirely. In either case, her goals will be essentially unchanged: Support new forms of global community, learn about new ways to use language, have some fun with communication.

We turn next to Chris Meier's fifth- and sixth-grade classroom in Tununak, Alaska. Students in Chris's class are the ones who corresponded with Ruth's students.

# 3

## Chris Meier's Fifth- and Sixth-Grade Classroom: Village Stories That Entertain and Teach

Alaska is large, sparsely populated, and inhabited by indigenous peoples who, having lived there for more than 1,000 years, are remarkably tolerant of the assortment of rugged individualists and misfits who have arrived during the last 2 centuries. It is instructive to read old journals of Russian Orthodox and Catholic missionaries alongside Raymond Carver (1992) stories to get a picture of the mix of transplants in Alaska. Residents in the "Lower 48," particularly in the Pacific Northwest, describe contemporary Alaska as the Frontier, the destination of choice for those who are tired of cities, traffic, and regulations.

Some, of course, have not escaped somewhere else. They have come to Alaska to live amidst unspoiled natural beauty, or they have come because of fossil fuels.

In 1968, great deposits of petroleum and natural gas were discovered in the Arctic coastal plain. Commercial oil production from these fields began in 1977, and today Alaska produces a significant percentage of U.S. oil. Petroleum from the fields is transported by an 800-mile-long pipeline to Valdez, where it is transferred to ocean-going tankers.

Most of us know considerably more about the pipeline and about Alaskan oil since March 1989, when the *Exxon Valdez* ran aground in Prince William Sound, spilling almost 11 million gallons of oil into the water, adversely affecting the marine system of humpback whales, salmon, seals, sea otters, and assorted bird species. Despite this catastrophe, the oil industry remains crucial to the state's economy. Education in Alaska is mostly funded by the state, and local districts suffer cutbacks when state oil royalties drop.

Even though Alaska is one of the least populated states in the United States, there are cities there. In fact, about three-fourths of the population of the state resides in Anchorage, Fairbanks, and Juneau (the state capital). However, the remaining one fourth, both indigenous peoples and transplants, lives in very small, very isolated towns and villages.

Tununak is one such village in western Alaska. The 325 or so Yup'ik Eskimos who live there are 300 miles from the nearest road, living on delta lowland criss-crossed with rivers and streams. To understand just how remote Tununak is, it helps to know that all of the children in the village were born in a public health service hospital in Bethel, the economic and flight hub for western Alaska. From Tununak, Bethel can be reached only by small open boat, small single-engine plane or, in winter, by snow machine.

A cash economy dependent on small-scale commercial herring and halibut fishing, and on the sale of skins and traditional craft items, is developing in Tununak, but subsistence hunting and fishing are still important for both cultural and material reasons. Members of families still fish and hunt together, and the catch of fish, sea mammals, and game animals is shared among them. Little boys still tell other little boys in Tununak that they want to be hunters when they grow up.

Hunting regulations are an example of two value systems in conflict in this part of Alaska. There has been a rapid decline in certain goose populations, resulting in a governmental prohibition against taking species during nesting and molting seasons. Apparently, the prohibition ended tremendously productive bird drives that were held into the 1970s. Anthropologist Ann Fienup-Riordan (1990) described events in which men, women, and children drove thousands of molting geese and goslings across the tundra, netted them, and then dispatched them by hand.

Federal Fish and Wildlife officials have met with Yup'ik tribal leaders to work out a compromise that involves prohibitions against spring hunting of some species, but not all. Fines and sanctions have been imposed for hunting protected species and for egg-gathering.

Some tensions remain: Geese have always been an important food source for the community, and many Yup'iks point to a long-held view that geese in this area are unlimited in number (essentially correct until recently). Also, even though officials blame hunters for most of the decline in the goose population, many Eskimos believe that biologists who set up observation platforms in the wetlands are harming the population by touching nests and creating trails that foxes can follow to raid the nests.

Despite incursions from elsewhere in North America and from Asia, despite the presence of a huge oil industry, and despite a federal presence in the form of hunting regulations, Tununak has an unusually strong hold on its native culture and language. Elders and their traditional teachings are respected. Youngsters learn important things, such as how to build a boat, by watching someone older and then copying that person's actions exactly. The family is important. Often, as many as eight persons—perhaps representing as many as four generations—live in a single house, with dozens of aunts, uncles, brothers, and sisters living only minutes away. Even though there are sources of English in the village—Rosemary Henze and Lauren Vanett (1993) reminded us that cable television is widely available, for example—Yup'ik is the language of the village for both adults and children.

In school, teachers (many of whom are nonnative and from the Lower 48) try to keep the culture and language alive for children, teaching, for instance, about traditional hunting and fishing, and about traditional crafts. Instruction is in Yup'ik until second grade and in English after that, but even in third grade and beyond, there is 1 hour per day of Yup'ik language instruction in school. A high school class produced a puppet show this year, taking myths, morals, and tales of warning told by the elders in Yup'ik and developing them for the stage. Their puppets were made of wood and clay and had traditional fur clothes made by the students. Their teacher, Hugh Dyment, reported that the class toured eight other villages "with a sort of Sesame Street performed in the native language."

## LIFE IN CHRIS MEIER'S FIFTH- AND SIXTH-GRADE CLASSROOM

Chris Meier is a teacher in his second year at Paul T. Albert Memorial School, the K–12 school in Tununak in which 95 students are enrolled. Someone somewhere probably still believes that teachers learn everything that they need to know in schools of education, that learning to teach is not a career-long process of knowing more, improving practice, and reflecting on both successes and failures, but teachers themselves know better. They know that much of what they learn emerges, as Herbert Kohl (1995) reminded us, from daily contact with students and from conversations with other teachers who are passionately involved in helping students learn.

Chris knows that in his second year of working with children, he still has a great deal to learn about teaching and learning.

Despite being very busy spending many hours planning lessons, Chris is intrigued by the idea of experimenting with Internet communication in his classroom. He is mindful of the isolation of the village, of the fact that there are no roads between villages, and that only one child of the 13 in his class has ever actually seen concrete. He wants his students to learn something about life outside of the village. He wants them to have opportunities to participate fully in the mainstream.

Another of his goals for his students is that they be biliterate, that they be able to interpret and compose large chunks of oral and written language in both Yup'ik and English. Discontinuities between village and school, and history of native languages in Alaska complicate this goal: Many older adults in Tununak use a Yup'ik orthography that was written by missionaries and is still found in church songbooks and deacons' Bibles. A modern Yup'ik orthography written by linguists at the Alaska Native Language Center at the University of Alaska, Fairbanks a little over 2 decades ago, one that Chris Meier described as "pure and logical," is not used by the older adults, but is the official version of written Yup'ik for schools. Chris reports that his fifth- and sixth-grade students are very proficient at reading and writing it. So the students in Chris Meier's class are literate in modern Yup'ik, but are able to use it, for the most part, only in school.

Henze and Vanett (1993) told us that many excellent written materials have been developed for the schools, but they are not usable by older generations, so older adults cannot assist children with their homework. In similar fashion, children cannot read the Bible written in the older orthography to aging family members.

With English, their second language, the children still struggle some. Both very recent research and rather old practice support the wisdom of asking learners to do considerable second-language speaking and writing for authentic purposes (e.g., corresponding on the Internet) to promote proficiency. Teachers can model language form, allow practice, and provide feedback. One of the most powerful demonstrations of this principle is Sylvia Ashton-Warner's (1986) work described in *Teacher*: For some 9 years, Ashton-Warner taught Maori children how to use their second language (English, just as in Tununak) by speaking and writing about themselves and about the drama in their lives.

Some writing of this sort can be sent over the Internet from Chris Meier's class because Tununak is oil-rich and, therefore, technology-rich. Oil royalties account for the bank of Macintoshes, the laser printer, and dedicated phone line for modem use available to Chris Meier and the other teachers and students.

Bertram C. Bruce and Andee Rubin (1993) noted that the most up-to-date technology is, in fact, available to Alaska's students. Isolation creates a need, and oil royalties provide the resources. Bruce and Rubin reported survey data from 1985 that showed Alaska leading the nation in the number of computers per student in public schools and, unlike other areas of the United States, there were few differences in availability of computers between large cities and tiny villages.

But more than computers are needed for telecommunications; an Internet service provider is essential. In *The New York Times*, Steve Lohr (1995) reported that America Online (AOL) is currently the nation's leading online computer service, with almost 5 million subscribers, each of whom pays a monthly fee. This population is about the size of metropolitan Atlanta or the state of Colorado. For much of the 1994–1995 year, Chris Meier's class relied on Hugh Dyment, the Tununak high school teacher with an AOL account, to help them send and receive messages. For about 15¢ a minute (20¢ during the day, 11¢ evenings and weekends), the class could call AOL in Washington State and access the Internet. After one of the younger children had composed a message on paper, a high school student usually assisted the child by typing the text into the computer. All messages received in Tununak were read aloud to the entire fifth- and sixth-grade class.

# MESSAGES FROM TUNUNAK:
# CONVERSATIONS WRITTEN DOWN

Earlier in this book, we mentioned that we like Shirley Brice Heath's (1983) phrase "conversations written down" as a description of Internet communication. The messages composed by the children in Chris Meier's class resemble, in many ways, the conversations that occur every day in the village. Language use is in accord with village cultural patterns (e.g., reserved, invariably polite). Chris Meier says he believes that the children think of their distant correspondents (the children whom we met in the last chapter, the children in Ruth Coleman's classroom in Joliet, Illinois) as conversational partners and that they think of the messages flowing to and from Tununak as conversations written down—a genre that makes perfect sense if one does not think of orality and literacy as wholly independent, mutually exclusive forms of language (and we do not). From the children's messages, we learn a great deal about village life.

## Village Topics

Topic choices, for instance, lean heavily toward matters of importance in the village—family and community (especially for the girls) and hunting (especially for the boys). Sally's and Gerald's first messages, sent to Illinois in mid-September, followed this pattern:

> . . . I am a Catholic. Is it cold there? On Friday we had a funeral, it was sad, even when they burried the body. . . . (Sally)

> I live in Tununak and I am a Yupik. I play basketball and we play football and sometimes we play lap game [a game similar to baseball brought to Alaska by reindeer herders from Lapland in the 1930s, and played with a bat and a soft ball; when a batter hits the ball, players attempt to run to the far end of a field and back without the opposing team hitting them with the ball]. And sometimes we go hunting with my big brother and Francis is my cousin. And sometimes I catch geese. Sometimes I go fishing and sometimes I watch cartoons and a scary movie. (Gerald)

About a month later, Chris Meier wrote a preface to the batch of messages sent from the children in Tununak: There is snow on the ground in Tununak now, temperatures are in the 30s, and 6 minutes of daylight are lost each day. The topics of the students' letters that followed are not substantially different from those sent in September. Again, we see a girl writing about family and community and a boy writing, at least in part, about hunting:

> . . . There was state troopers in town yesterday. They were looking for people because they broke the law. . . . (Elizabeth A.)

> . . . It is going to snow here and I am glad, super glad. You know why? I want to go ptarmigan hunting [a ptarmigan is a grouse, a bird with completely feathered feet that lives in northern regions] and ski-doo riding, even seld riding and make snowmen, and even make an avalanche in the snow. . . . (Jeffrey)

In early December, boys and girls alike wrote from Tununak about fierce animals and hunting adventures. However, we still see details about family and community creeping into the girls' messages:

. . . There are dangerous animals here like fox, wolf, mink, wesels and other animals. I am a boy. I would not go near them because they can kill us right away. (Jeffrey)

. . . here theres musk ox and we eat musk ox there delisous. Here I play Lap game, baseball, dubbel dutch, and bike around in summer. I have 9 familys. I have 5 sisters and 2 brothers and a mom and a dad and uncle and aunties and grandma's and grandpa's. . . . (Margaret)

. . . We saw lot's of muskox they were close to the school our school's name is Paul. T. Albert Memoial School. We have 10 class rooms our school is almost big. I never saw any alive muskox close-up, only dead ones. But I saw one far away. . . . (Grace)

. . . Today we went out for a fresh air, but all of staid in the porch. What are you girls going to sing in Christmas? We are going to sing Up On The House Top. Did you know there is musk ox here? When my class mates whet by the hill we saw some musk ox up on the hill. . . . (Stacy)

When my dad and I went hunting ptarmigan, I caught three ptarmigan. By the hill, my dad and I saw four hawks attacking the ptarmigan. The ptarmigan was going fast and the hawk was going faster. The other hawks were looking for the other ptarmigan. But the hawks could not find a ptarmigan. My Dad and I went to look for some ptarmigan. I saw a ptarmigan. But we did not shoot the ptarmigan because it was going fast. (David)

## Telling Stories

David's story about hunting ptarmigan is stunning in its detail. Like the Roadville children's stories that Shirley Brice Heath (1983) described, David's story is a "true" story, one based on actual events involving important characters (his father, himself, and the birds), and the images, created in part by the detail that David includes, help David's readers imagine the scene by the hill. The details make the story, as Deborah Tannen (1989) noted, clustering, as they often do, at story beginnings (how many ptarmigan were caught? three) and ends (what happened? Dad and I went to look for ptarmigan, and we saw one, but we didn't shoot it, because it was going fast).

In all likelihood, David conjured up an image of what happened there while he composed the story. The children in Illinois (and we) can also create an image in our minds as part of trying to make sense of what we read.

Details create intimacy. Note Deborah Tannen's (1989, p. 150) example of "His bed was undisturbed" versus "The chenille spread tucked properly around the pillow." The former conveys the fact that someone is not at home, but the latter conveys the image of the unslept-in bed, rather than just the idea of it. In the same way, Grace could write simply that the rock people are piles of rocks on which one can climb (the idea). Instead, she writes with such detail that what reaches her Illinois audience is image, as well as idea:

> The rock people are just a pile of rocks, flat rocks. If you go up you will see the whole village and the pond and ocean. And you will be scared. At the rock people it is cool. If you go down to the village after you were cold, and if you go down it will be hot.

If Grace's narrative voice is full of wonder, David's in his story about hunting ptarmigan is almost breathless. His word choice of "fast" in one form or another, repeated throughout the short story, sets our pace, and we race through a reading: " . . . By the hill, my dad and I saw four hawks attacking the ptarmigan. The ptarmigan was going fast and the hawk was going faster. . . ."

David's story is similar to the tales that entertain and teach, told by the elders in the village. Hugh Dyment reminded us that in traditional Yup'ik culture, learning takes place when someone young imitates the actions of someone older. David is learning about telling a story that the elders might tell: a reality-based tale, involving the teller, adhering to actual order of events, and sometimes (but not always) including an interpretation of the meaning of the events recounted.

Elizabeth K. is not quite so adept as David (she refers to both a red scarf and to "Jahnathan" that we, her readers, can only find unclear), but again she tells a reality-based tale, involving herself, with clearly ordered actions:

> . . . A long time me and some friend went up the hill. We put the red scarf on. then the mask ox was going to come. They attacked us. But we hid Jahnathan on the grass. Then that jumped on it, then the boy jumped off the ground.

And, Spencer does exactly the same, telling a reality-based tale, involving himself, adhering to order (again including a father as a central character and, again, setting a breathless pace with the word "fast"):

. . . In Tununak is fun and not fun. My Dad and I went to Toksook Bay by ski-doo. When my dad went fast, I went fast too. When we went home I had no gas and oil. My Dad had gas and oil. My brother and I went to go catch football and basketball. We never played basketball and we had no ball and bat. . . .

What is it about stories? They chronicle events, convey universal truths, reach out and grab us as readers, making us feel as if we are confronting something familiar even if the events are quite novel, quite out of our range of experience (e.g., hunting ptarmigan, happening on a musk ox, for many of us). This powerful reaction to stories seems to occur for short, simple stories, like those written in Tununak, as well as for long, complex narratives with obscure motivation among characters, inverted order of events, and multiple subplots.

In *Acts of Meaning*, Jerome Bruner (1990) wrestled with this question of the power of stories, of why they have such a grip on the human imagination. He listed some essential properties of all stories: (a) sequentiality (David, Elizabeth K., and Spencer all understand this property); (b) "factual indifference," which is to say that they can be real or imaginary (the three children opt for real); (c) a forging of links between the exceptional and the ordinary (this is part of what Sylvia Ashton-Warner celebrates: children writing about their daily lives but, as it turns out, lives with great drama in them); and (d) dramatism itself, including actors, actions, goals, and so on (again, David, Elizabeth K., and Spencer have plenty of these in their stories). And, stories are often (e) simultaneously concrete and metaphoric.

Also, (f) they are, in each case, *somebody's* story. There is a narrator's voice, events are seen from the narrator's perspective (e.g., " . . . If you go up you will see the whole village and the pond and ocean, . . . " " . . . When my dad went fast, I went fast too . . . ").

A truly overriding property, according to Bruner, is that stories resist logical procedures for establishing what they mean. As we said earlier, they must be interpreted. This of course means that they are open to diverse interpretations from listeners and readers: Were Elizabeth K.'s characters timid or brave? Did Spencer tell a tale of exciting events, or one of reckless behavior and poor judgment? And what was the reason why David and his father never took aim at the last ptarmigan? The "gists" of stories simply cannot be extracted unambiguously.

Bruner so believed in the power of narrative that he defined a cultural community like Tununak, not only in terms of shared beliefs about what people are like, what the world is like, and what has value, but also in terms of narrative means for explicating crisis and conflict. We tell stories, in part, because they help us explain behavior that is difficult to understand in other ways. Perhaps this is what Jeffrey, Margaret, Grace, Stacy, and David were doing when they wrote messages in early December—telling stories about fierce animals, so that their fear was understandable—to themselves and to others. (We do tell stories to ourselves, of course. Bruner noted that these stories are told for much the same reason as the stories that we tell others are—not simply to report, but to make sense of everyday life.)

Anne Lamott (1994), author rather than psychologist, says some of the same things about stories: When people write a little every day (as the children in Chris Meier's classroom do), they end up writing about the drama of humankind. Most truly great writing reveals who we are to some degree. Life is complicated, and we grapple with events that can be confusing (e.g., adults breaking the law) and terrifying (e.g., hunting dangerous animals). Sometimes writers are so gifted that they can shed a little light on these events.

## Asking Questions

We noticed that the children writing from Illinois to Tununak asked many questions—not the formulaic questions that Shirley Brice Heath (1983) described when a parent coaches a child to pay attention to an event ("What's that? Who's coming? You hear Daddy's car?") and not the "teacher" questions that Courtney Cazden (1988) discussed, when a teacher asks a student only questions to which she already knows the answer ("What time is it, Sarah?" "Half-past two." "Right."), but real, child-formulated questions. The children in Illinois asked about the weather, about favorite colors and sports, about vacations, about pets, and about book bags and homework.

The children in Chris Meier's class asked considerably fewer questions: Of the 56 questions posed by any child between early September and early October, 52 of them were asked by children in Illinois. Of the 13 children in Illinois who wrote during the month, 11 asked at least one question, whereas only 2 of 8 children writing from Tununak asked questions. There were individual differences within classrooms, of course, but the differences between classrooms were dramatic. What we observed, in other words, was what Deborah Tannen (1989) noted: Cultural patterns establish a range within which individuals vary. Or, as Robert LeVine (1982) put it, culture is an organizer of goals, purposes, and intentions for individuals.

Chris Meier is married to a Yup'ik woman, has lived in Tununak for 4 years at the time of this writing, and has a good deal of specific knowledge about the culture and language of his students. He helped us understand how village conversations operate, and that, in turn, has helped us understand why the children's messages to Illinois included relatively few questions. Chris told us that Tununak children have very little experience with people from outside of the village. The people they meet are almost always from very near-by, and questions about their interests and activities are not particularly necessary.

Chris also told us that when a Yup'ik meets another Yup'ik whom he or she does not know, the person will try immediately to establish a linkage through a family member or friend in common. Interconnectedness of Yup'ik society and valuing of ancestry mean that a linkage can usually be found. In the rare instance in which a person in common cannot be found, the person encountered is truly a stranger. Strangers are welcomed in the village and listened to, but seldom questioned. Questioning a stranger would be considered impolite.

In the context of asking questions, many of the fifth- and sixth-grade children did something very interesting, something that Chris suggested be edited out of the messages that were eventually sent to Illinois, so we only know about this from him: They included in their early messages long lists of their family members. These lists were most likely an attempt to establish a family linkage with their correspondents, much as would be attempted in a face-to-face conversation with a stranger. Chris told us that three or four of the students included lists of as many as 10 names!

The decision that Chris Meier made—suggesting to his students that they delete their lists of names—reminds us of Katherine Merseth's (1992) point that actions taken by teachers to alleviate one dilemma may exacerbate another. Chris wanted his students to be involved with their correspondents, to avoid confusing them. However, in concentrating on this goal, he altered the children's words—a practice of which many researchers of effective teaching for ethnic- and language-minority students would disapprove. Kenneth Zeichner (1993) urged that teachers support students' cultural identity. Linda Levine (1993) argued that teachers must recognize, make room for, and build on the verbal and nonverbal resources that children bring to school. In Tununak, one of these resources is the children's knowledge of the village practice of initiating a conversation with a stranger by attempting to find family members or friends in common.

## Brevity

Brevity is also part of conversational practice in Tununak. Both Chris Meier and Hugh Dyment commented on Tununak conversations: In a Yup'ik home, the family members are reserved with one another. Words and language are believed to be very powerful—something to be used gingerly. Hugh told us that there "isn't a lot of chit chat between people when there isn't specific reason for it," particularly between adults and children. Affection is expressed in other ways.

This pattern of conciseness of expression emerges in the children's messages to Illinois. For example, just after the start of the school year, a boy in Illinois, Tad, wrote a long, chatty message to Tununak, full of questions about weather and clothing:

> . . . It is around 80 degrees here in the daytime now. How about there? Is there snow always up there? We wear shorts and T-shirts to school now. Later, it will get chilly as Fall comes, and Winter. Then we will wear warmer clothes. What do you wear? Soon the trees will turn beautiful bright colors. Then the leaves fall off. . . .

The responses from four girls in Chris Meier's class were substantially shorter, more to the point:

> . . . I am slways using jackets to school and clothes. . . . (Elizabeth A.)

> . . . In winter I wear snow pants. . . . (Elizabeth K.)

> . . . 55 degrees today. . . . (Stacy)

> . . . I have a Parka, but it is used in winter time. . . . (Grace)

(These clipped, concise responses are also consistent with our assuming that the children thought of the Internet exchanges as conversations written down. When a person asks, "Did you see the mystery on PBS last night?" the face-to-face respondent does not need to say, "In response to your question about the mystery, I did not see it." He or she simply says, "yes" or "no." The four responses about weather and clothing resemble a conversational chain that might occur in the village.)

An even sharper contrast in chattiness occurred in an exchange between Jadine, an avid writer in Illinois, and Tommy in Tununak. Jadine wrote a very long message addressed to Stacy, a student in Chris Meier's class with whom she had already exchanged one set of messages. Embedded in her message were many questions about rock people, sleep-overs, school buses, and movie theaters:

> . . . I would love to live in Alaska. We still do not understand what are your "rock people?" Please explain more about them. We are dying to figure this out! Have you ever had a sleep over? that is when your

girlfriends come over to your house to sleep over night. We play games and we stay up late and watch TV, and talk and giggle a lot. Wouldn't it be neat if we could have a sleep over? Have you ever ridden on a yellow school bus? I ride on one every day to and from school. It is fun because you meet new people. It is noisy, but you get used to it. My birthday was last Sunday. I went to Shoney's. That is a food restaurant here. I went to Toys R Us and bought a make-up kit.

Then I went to a movie, "Camp Nowhere." Do you have a movie theater? This Saturday my family will celebrate with a party at my Grandmother's house. After we eat, we kids will go to the park to play. Tell me how you celebrate birthdays. . . .

Somewhat unexpectedly, after this message was read aloud to the entire class, Tommy, not Stacy, replied. His responses are considerably more abbreviated than Jadine's inquiries; few words are wasted:

The rock people are just stacks of rocks. There is about tem rock rock people. NO! I never had a sleep over. Yes I did ride a yellow school bus. A long time ago there used to be a theater but it was with film strips. Now we have cable TV and a video store.

We agree with Chris Meier and Hugh Dyment that there are really two important reasons for brevity in the messages from Tununak: First, conciseness of expression is one feature of conversational patterns in the village, acquired by the children simply because they live in the village, listen to adult models for conversation, and then converse themselves. In Tununak, this sort of adult modeling and holistic acquisition by children applies to language and to many other aspects of village life. When the children came to compose for the Illinois children, they employed the acquired pattern of brevity.

A second reason for brevity is that the children in Chris Meier's class are writing in their second language, with which, as we said earlier, they still struggle some. It is seldom the case that children are equally adept in first and second language, and Chris tells us that this is so for his students: They are generally 3 to 5 years behind in English language development when compared with children who acquired English as their first language. (He also told us that great second-language leaps are made by many students, an excellent example being two Tununak students who graduated recently from high school, attended college, and then returned to the village, endorsements in hand, to teach.) For the fifth and sixth graders who are struggling with their second language, one would expect that they would write less in that language, not more.

# ARE THERE BENEFITS
# IN CORRESPONDING ACROSS CULTURES?

Chris Meier wanted his fifth- and sixth-grade students to learn something about life outside of the village in which they live. What did they learn by writing to students in Joliet, Illinois, and what did the Illinois students learn from the exchanges?

Surely, some cultural stereotypes yielded to more accurate information. For example, the Illinois children seemed quite comfortable initially with the movie image of all Eskimos living in igloos near glacial fjords (despite the fact that Yup'ik Eskimos live on soggy tundra, rather than on snow and ice).

Betsey's question from Illinois in early September leads us to believe that she probably accepted the stereotypic view:

> . . . I wanted to know if any Eskimo children you know, live in Igloos?

And, even though Elizabeth A. wrote right back from Tununak to clarify, with

> . . . I do not know any children live in igloos . . . ,

Edward in Illinois joined the discussion, clinging to the stereotype, rather than acknowledging Elizabeth A.'s information:

> . . . For fun do you make igloos? . . .

Furthermore, Betsey wrote again, on the same day as Edward, offering the following comments:

> . . . Today we might build a model igloo out of sugar cubes. When it is winter me and some of my friends are going to build an igloo out of snow and ice. I have never tried to build an igloo before. . . .

If the children in Illinois understood that some Eskimos do not live in igloos, why was a model being built, and why did Betsey mention to her Yup'ik correspondent that they were going to build an igloo when winter arrived?

Our explanation is rather straightforward: As we said elsewhere (Garner & Hansis, 1994), we all, children and adults alike, use stereotypes without awareness. When we do not have the corrective of sustained contact with groups of people different from ourselves, we are likely to rely on expectations and images from our limited experience. We all have what Howard Gardner (1991) called "habits of the mind" (p. 4) that get in the way of thorough-going understanding of other people and their actions.

A corrective occurred, though, because the children in Tununak and Illinois corresponded over time, and during the winter they prepared videotapes to send to each other. In the tape that Chris Meier prepared, we see the children, the school, the play area, the old and new sections of the village, the rock people (mentioned in the children's messages), and the ocean. One of the first things that the narrator of the video (Chris Meier) asks the children is "What is that behind you?" to which they respond, in chorus, "the tundra." There is little snow, no ice and, of course, no igloos.

The children in Illinois who viewed the video could not help but notice that Tununak differs from Illinois (28° in early October, we are told by the narrator; sun low in the sky, wind blowing the children's hair as they play lap game on the play deck), but it is not all snow and ice. In addition, if they expected that their Tununak correspondents would be clothed exclusively in animal skins and fur, that image too was disconfirmed: The children wear jeans, letter jackets, and light parkas (in other words, exactly what the Illinois children wear).

Cultural stereotypes were dispelled in the other direction as well. Hugh Dyment tells us that students in Tununak assume that all citizens in the Lower 48 experience violent crime on a daily basis, and that they are heavily armed—not for hunting, but for self-defense. The students see just enough news and entertainment on cable television to be certain that this is probably so (even if they would surely consider it impolite to ask the Illinois children if they have been victimized and if they have weapons in their homes). The video sent from Illinois, showing a small school in a quiet neighborhood, provides a different, more accurate, image.

It is possible that erosion of cultural stereotypes through sustained contact and exchange of ideas—in both text and visual image—can assist us in working toward the goal of affirming plurality and difference. One of the first steps in our doing that, as Maxine Greene (1993) noted, may be learning to hear each other's stories. Children in Tununak and Illinois are writing some of these stories now—about themselves and about the drama in their lives.

In chapter 4, we tell another Tununak story. This time, we look at Internet communication to and from Hugh Dyment's high school students.

# 4

# Hugh Dyment's High School Classroom: Talk Between Equals

Tununak, Alaska, as we said in the last chapter, is a tiny Yup'ik Eskimo village 300 miles from the nearest road. It sits on the Bering Sea coast, and inhabitants are dependent in large measure on subsistence hunting for sea and game animals and on fishing.

It is a village with a strong hold on its native culture and language, despite some Western influences—nonnative teachers from the "Lower 48" for one. One of the teachers who has come to the village is Hugh Dyment who, at the time of this writing, has been in Tununak for 4 years and in Alaska off and on since 1987. He holds a degree in political science along with a teaching endorsement. Hugh teaches high school classes in the village.

## LIFE IN HUGH DYMENT'S HIGH SCHOOL CLASSROOM

Hugh Dyment knows and values the culture and language of both worlds, Yup'ik and Western. His Yup'ik daughter was given two names—a Yup'ik one (Kakaaq, after her maternal great-grandmother) and a Christian one (Mary). Hugh and his family eat what others in the village eat, including raw and frozen halibut, trout and blackfish, raw seal, walrus liver, and seagull eggs. Hugh hunts and fishes with family members and knows how to build boats and repair snow machines, just as the other men in Tununak do. It was Hugh who took the lead in producing a school puppet show this year that relied on myths, morals, and tales of warning told in Yup'ik by the village elders. His high school class made puppets of wood and clay, clothed in fur. With him, the class traveled to eight other villages to perform.

Hugh also recognizes the need for Tununak high school students to make a transition from speaking and writing in only their first language (Yup'ik) to speaking and writing fluently in their second language (English) as well. This is especially important for those who will leave the village soon to attend college. This goal of English fluency for the high school students is not the "compensatory" goal discussed by Olga Romero (1994), in which children and adolescents are assisted in getting rid of their first language as quickly as possible and are made to feel stigmatized if the shift to English occurs too slowly.

On the contrary, in Tununak, truly bilingual, bicultural education exists. The approach fits Joel Spring's (1994) description: Students from a dominated group are taught how to maintain their own cultural traditions and, at the same time, are taught how to act in the dominant culture. Both native language maintenance and fluency in English are valued. School instruction occurs in English after second grade, but there is still 1 hour per day of Yup'ik language instruction in third grade and beyond.

One important way in which Hugh promotes fluency in English among his students is by providing them an opportunity to communicate, in English, over the Internet. This Internet activity is not the decontextualized skill-oriented work often experienced by language-minority students. Instead, it is authentic communication, rich in meaning-making and interaction possibilities. As Jim Cummins and Dennis Sayers (1995) pointed out, *asynchronous* communication (communication that does not occur in real time) allows second-language learners extra time to seek assistance and polish responses—time that they would not have in face-to-face conversation or timed writing for a teacher.

Because oil royalties have made possible strong state support of technology in Alaskan schools, Hugh's classroom has a handful of Macintoshes, a laser printer, and a dedicated phone line for modem use. Hugh and his students can call AOL in Washington State to access the Internet. They can chat, live, with teenagers all over the country. They can also send written messages to peers and to adults who have moved from the village. Each contact provides students with practice communicating in English.

In the written messages, which we have read, the students themselves have determined when they will write, to whom they will write, and what they will write. Hugh assists them, as the need arises, in locating e-mail addresses. Peers act as editors. Interest is high.

As an aside, we should repeat something that we said many pages back, namely that this policy of letting students speak and write during large chunks of each school day, choosing their audience and topic, is quite a departure from typical classroom practice. In most classrooms, as Courtney Cazden (1988) reminded us, there is an obvious asymmetry in classroom talk: Whereas teachers may speak at any time and to any person, filling any silence and interrupting any speaker, using any volume or tone of voice that they choose, students may not. Students may choose to be compliant, may participate in whispered private utterances, or they may simply "tune out." As for classroom writing, it is usually accompanied by time and topic constraints, and a teacher's grade plus a good dose of what Frank Smith (1986) characterized as exercises and drills about writing, rather than actual writing. Hugh Dyment's class is quite different from this.

The teenagers in Hugh's class speak and write a great deal. And, what they write is interesting and coherent. We attribute much of the interestingness in their messages to the choices that they have been given; they, not their teacher, as we have said, select both audience and topic. We agree with Ann Renninger (1992) that personal interest in a topic evokes increased attention and effort. Why, we have wondered a bit more, are the second-language messages so coherent, so clearly linked to what their correspondents have written?

Roger Schank and Richard Osgood (1993) gave us an idea about this. Schank and Osgood have written about the role of stories in conversation, and their analysis is useful if we continue to think about Internet communication as conversations written down—that is, as language use that sits between orality and literacy, more like speaking than writing in its use of an informal, interactive style but more like writing than speaking in that messages are composed, stored on electronic disks, and sent over computer networks to be read on computer screens.

Schank and Osgood described conversations as follows: In a conversation between us, understanding requires that you map your stories onto my stories. We take turns telling our respective stories. Coherence in a conversation occurs when the story that I tell makes sense after you tell yours. A listener with many stories pays attention to a conversational partner in order to select from his or her repertoire a story that is most connected to the other person's story. Understanding is figuring out which story, of many, to tell.

Actually, Roger Schank and Chip Cleary (1994) made it clear that this analysis is intended to explain more than conversation. They argued that much human reasoning is case based, rather than rule based, that when people solve problems, they frequently recall problems of a similar nature that they have faced previously. Think about picking the most efficient check-out line at the supermarket or about dealing with a mechanic who disagrees with your assessment that your car still rattles or trying to find just the right gift for a curmudgeonly parent. We constantly search our memories for old information that might help us process new information. Being educated, according to Schank and Cleary, means having access to a wealth of cases—stories—with which to solve new problems.

We accept this analysis, and think that, in terms of conversation, whether or not one has a history of telling stories to a particular conversational partner might make a difference in the coherence of the conversations that occur. If, for example, one of us speaks and writes to a good friend over many years, she already knows some of the characters in my stories (my sister, my husband), some of the past plots (adolescent mischief, marriages, moves both personal and professional), and she knows my voice, my general perspective on persons and events. The flow in our conversation should be good as we tell new stories on top of old, with some elements maintained and with expectations in hand about where our stories will connect. This is exactly what we see in the correspondence between Tununak teenagers in Hugh Dyment's class and adults who have left the village. It is that correspondence that we examine in some detail here.

# CORRESPONDING WITH FAVORITE ADULTS: NEW STORIES ON TOP OF OLD

Father Delmore is a priest who lived for a time in Tununak and was well liked by the high school students. He is living in Seattle now, and it is there that messages were sent to him.

## Correspondence With Father Delmore

One message to Father Delmore was a rather choppy note, but one in which a teenager, Samuel, makes an obvious effort to link events in Tununak and Seattle, mentioning characters who are familiar to the priest:

Dear Father Delmore,

Hello, how are you? My name is Walter Samuel Walter. Hey, I don't know what God's name is, can you tell me his real name? Father Delmore, remember me? I'm Peter Walter and Susie Walter's son. I was born on the 28th of September 1978 I am 16 years old right now. So what are you doing down at Seattle? Is the weather at Seattle always warm?

Do they have church at Seattle? Here at Tununak the weather has been warm and cold. What apartment do you stay in. Do you watch the Seattle Supersonics play Basketball? How many people is there in Seattle.

Father Delmore's response is chatty and informal. In it, he tells his stories that connect to Samuel's: If Tununak weather has fluctuated between warm and cold, Seattle weather has been rainy, and, in response to a direct query from Samuel, yes, he watches the Sonics at his mother's house on pay-for-view television. In addition, like Samuel, Father Delmore attempts a connection by mentioning family:

. . . Yes I remember you and your family. Be sure to say hello to your mother and father for me.

I'm taking a few theology courses here at Seattle U and getting "rested and renewed" for the future. The weather is warm today in the 50s and it was raining earlier. And how bout those Sonics, huh? Pretty good team this year. I watch them on "pay for view" t.v. at my mothers sometimes.

Take care of yourself.

Schank and Osgood's (1993) point that someone selects from his or her repertoire a story that is most connected to the other person's story is demonstrated when Father Delmore receives a second message that reads like a printed-out internal dialogue—a sweet message from Bobbiann, with stories about shyness during confirmation class and worries related to making a college decision:

Hello, hello. How are you doing? I thought you might be interested of how Tununak is doing.

Well first of all, Tununak is doing great. Juniors and Seniors and some young adults are getting ready for confirmation. We take classes every Wednesday evening for two hours. Some young adults who are joining us are taking classes with us because they weren't confirmed last year or the past years. During our first class with Dick Lincoln, Sophie Oscar, and Father Peter, we were too quiet. I guess we were too shy to ask questions because it was our first time, and we just sat there and listened to Father Peter's lecture. Maybe when we get to know Father Peter, I guess we'll get to ask more questions. [A long paragraph about church retreats comes next.]

Last of all, my school is doing just fine. Since I am a senior, I'm planning to go to college. But I first need to make up one more credit in order for me to graduate and get my diploma. That means I have to back to school and take just one class that I have failed during the past years of my high school. I haven't really decided where to go to college because there are so many places I'd like to go. Some of my friends are going to Sheldon Jackson College and some of them are going to Anchorage. I don't know where I'd like to go, but I'd like to go where I feel comfortable and able to learn something about the outside world.

If you have time, I would appreciate hearing from you. . . .

Bobbiann's description of the confirmation class would have rich meaning for Father Delmore (who preceded Father Peter in working with the Tununak students), so she has selected her story well. In addition, her story about college and uncertainty seems designed to elicit exactly the response about college that comes, given the priest's general perspective on persons and events ("Take advantage of the college opportunities"):

. . . I hit the jackpot today, getting all of these fine letters from different students. Be sure to say hello to you Mom for me, I hear she is taking good care of Fr. Peter the new priest. I hope his health is holding up with his fasting for the village.

Sounds like you have some good plans for the future, and I hope you take advantage of the college opportunities. . . .

Father Delmore adds a story of his own (Father Peter is fasting "for the village"), again a story chosen well, for it is Bobbiann's mother who is looking after Father Peter.

It is interesting to see that both of these exchanges with Father Delmore represent what A. D. Edwards and D. P. G. Westgate (1994) described as "talk between equals." Neither participant has special rights or responsibilities, both have obligations to tell stories that connect to the other person's. Adults and children or adolescents often engage in communication in which one participant is more knowledgeable or more in control (usually the adult) and one is less knowledgeable or less in control (usually the child or adolescent), but these exchanges do not follow that pattern, for just as Father

Delmore has connecting stories to tell (about theology courses, the Sonics, the rain, and the new priest in Tununak), so too do Samuel and Bobbiann (about the weather, confirmation class, and plans for college).

Three elements in particular seem to contribute to an impression of talk between equals: *informality* (e.g., the priest's "how bout those Sonics, huh?" to Samuel); *humor* (e.g., "I hit the jackpot today" from Father Delmore to Bobbiann); and, most important perhaps, a substantial amount of *self-disclosure* from all participants. For instance, Bobbiann tells Father Delmore that she wants to go to college "where I feel comfortable and able to learn something about the outside world," and Father Delmore reveals that he watches the Sonics on television at his mother's home (a small, but personal, detail) and that he is concerned about Father Peter's fasting.

Students in Hugh's class also wrote to a well-liked couple who taught at one time in Tununak. The teachers, Doug and Julie, now live in Bend, Oregon, with their young daughter.

## Correspondence With Doug and Julie

The first message to Doug and Julie was from Sebastian Oscar and Anthony. In the message, the boys tell stories that would make sense to their former teachers—stories about grades, talking in class, athletics, and graduation:

Hi! Greetings from Sebastian and Anthony. So far we are doing good in school and our grades seems to be better than last time. We have been good students too, but sometimes some of the student talk a lot.

We have been doing good in basketball also, but we placed third in the District Tournament in Bethel, which is not good. It was not good because Toksook won the tournament, we were a better team, but we lost against them. Tell you the truth we had that game in our hands and just let it slip. We were leading the game by 7 points with two minutes to go, we had some turn overs going on and it came to a point where they led by 3, then we lost by that number. It was a huge upset for the Coaster boy's team. Over all the LKSD basketball teams, we had the highest G.P.A. It was the only trophy we Coaster boys brought home. I "S" also took home an All-Tournament Team pin, so did my bro, Harry.

Tununak's doing just fine. . . . [this punctuation from the original]. when was the last time you saw him? I joke! Tununak to us is same old, same old. But there are some dances in the week ends. [A section naming all graduating seniors appears next.]

I guess that's all folks?

Just as in the exchanges with Father Delmore, this note is clearly talk between equals. Once again, there is informality—some of it colloquial English, perhaps mimicking cable television dialogue to which most of the teenagers in Tununak have access (e.g., "Hi," "we had that game in our hands and just let it slip," "so did my bro, Harry," "same old, same old," and the closing "I guess that's all folks?"). There is humor, marked as such: "Tununak's doing just fine.... when was the last time you saw him? I joke!" And, once again, there is self-disclosure when Sebastian and Anthony reveal to their former teachers that some of the students are chattering in class; that their basketball team should have won, but let the game slip away; and that the routine of the village is broken by weekend dances.

What is so striking about the this self-disclosure is that the boys did not need to reveal any of these details. In telling the story of the basketball game, they could have added some self-aggrandizing piece about the other team being bigger or tougher or about the officials favoring the other side. Instead, they let it be known that they had "blown" the game. (They do manage, rather shyly we think, to slip in the detail of the All-Tournament Team pins that were awarded to Sebastian and Harry.)

The story of the basketball game provides a good example of what we mean by "new stories on top of old." After all, Doug and Julie know the characters in this particular story (Sebastian, Anthony, Harry, and the rest of the Tununak team), they know something about past plots (in this case, the athletic rivalry between Tununak and Toksook), and they know the voice of the storyteller (Sebastian, who candidly admits blowing the game, but then shyly slips in the detail of the pin awarded him). Sebastian and Anthony have chosen to tell a story that connects to Doug and Julie's past experiences in Tununak. It is familiar and comprehensible.

Other messages were sent to Doug and Julie from students in Hugh Dyment's class, and these messages are similar in that they too are new stories on top of old. When Sebastian Post writes, he tells the former teachers, among other things, that there have been some changes in the school building, changes that Sebastian is upset about and that he knows that Doug and Julie will understand (Doug, after all, taught carpentry in the now-closed shop classroom):

... Doug, There is no more wood shop for any of us, because there is no Voc. Ed. teacher and that is a bore. Since there is no teacher for that class, it has become dangerous to operate all of the equipment without any supervisor. Myself, I'm afraid to operate the equipment, but I have operated them sometimes and it ain't that bad.

The other thing about school is that the dark room has been clean out. Now, it has become the student store, and we are doing well in selling pop and confections.

I am doing fine, but I miss the carpentry class that we had when you were here. . . .

The next message, a chatty one from William Charlie, connects more with Julie, rather than with Doug. William selects stories to tell that link to Julie's science teaching in Tununak and to her concern that the students finish high school. In addition, he connects the story of a new adoption in his family to his inquiry about Doug and Julie's child:

. . . Hey Julie, just to let you know, things are doing great in school so far. You want to know why? We didn't have our science class yet! As usual, things will go down when science starts, right? You should know Julie [Hugh tells us that William's only "D" in high school was in Julie's science class].

How's little Elin? I heard she started walking. Guess what? We adopted a baby boy about three months ago. We named him Evertt Andy Charlie. FIRST Evertt in town! Well, he's a pain, but he's cute and charming like any other baby.

It's getting close to the end of the schoo year. I can't wait. Also, only 6 out of 9 Seniors are going to graduate., and only 6 are going to Hawaii for the Pacific Rim Close-Up. this year, things are going wrong, don't you think? [Information about school tournaments follows.]

Like a disease, the seniors have Senioritous. Seniors getting clumsy, always late, hardly any homeworks turned in on time. You know what I'm talking about, right. That's one of the problems we're starting to have. SENIORITOUS!

Seems like since you left Julie, our school has lost it's spirit. Even the student council representatives have nothing to do make this school year fun.

William makes explicit what we have been calling new stories on top of old when he remarks that "As usual, things will go down when science starts, right? You should know Julie" and "You know what I'm talking about, right. That's one of the problems we're starting to have. SENIORITOUS!" William acknowledges with these comments that he and Julie have a shared history in Tununak.

When Doug and Julie respond to the messages from Tununak, they match the students' informality, humor, and self-disclosure (even elaborating on a harrowing time in the mountains and revealing that Doug did not get his substitute-teaching application in promptly). In other words, we are once again seeing talk between equals. Doug and Julie also select from all the stories that they might tell about life in Oregon the ones most connected to the stories that the Tununak students have told:

Hello men!

Good to hear from the Coasters. We really liked getting all of your letters. They each had something very interesting to share. We were a little shocked to hear that only 6 of the seniors are graduating, but we are sure that those who aren't will get their act together so they can enjoy life after high school. [A discussion of a vacation in Arizona at Julie's parents' home follows.]

Doug got to do lots of hiking in the Catalina mountains. One day he went for a 16 mile hike. He was going to call Julie when he was finished but when he didn't call by 6:00 p.m., she went looking for him. Good thing he learned all those survival skills in Tununak because he ended up spending the night up in the mountains. He had to build a shelter to sleep in and a fire going to keep the bobcats and mountain lions away. Julie's family was relieved to have him back home the next day. [A section on building a new house comes next.]

S.P. spoke of missing the woodshop. Doug also misses that place. His odd collection of tools, and no indoor workshop, is going to make it hard to build cabinets for the kitchen. He brags to all of his friends about what good woodworkers you guys were. It's clear he really misses teaching that class. . . .

Julie has been the "bread winner" in the family lately. She was more organized and got her substitute teaching application in right away so she has been teaching fairly regularly. She says that the kids down here are sometimes more disrespectful of their teachers, but then, sub's never really do get much respect. When julie goes away to teach, Doug stays home and watches Elin. Elin still calls Doug "Mom." . . .

Two more messages were sent to Doug and Julie—a group message written on the same day that the long note about hiking, woodworking, and substitute teaching was received, and a short note from Priscilla. Both pose a question, awkwardly, about Julie's being pregnant (the "p" word is never used, however!). The group wrote first:

Hello again!

Well, just read the letter to the whole class and there were a few laughs here and there. . . .

This is to you Julie. The whole class has been hearing some rumors that you're . . . you know. Something that's similar to Elin. So they wanted me to ask you. Only if you know what I mean.

You guys should send a picture of Elin. We'll make a deal with you, if you send us a picture of all you three, all seniors will send an individual cap and gown picture of themselves. DEAL? Okay, deal. . . .

The next day, Priscilla converted rumor to fact, with more questions for Julie:

Hi Julie,

It's me Priscilla Post. How are you? Me doing fine here in Tununak. I heard your getting another baby in two months. Boy! That's amazing!!!!!!!!!! What do you expect it to be? A boy or another girl? My sister got back Denver, Colorado. She went over there to baby-sit for my Auntie Mary. Will you ever come here because I want to see your baby. My big brother is going to have collage at Anchorage for about to years then come back. He might get married to Marjorie George if he has the guts to ask her to marry her.

I hope I don't fail health class because I'm not donig good. The first nine weeks I got 4.0 then got 3.8 on the second nine weeks. . . .

Because all of the correspondents in this sequence of messages have selected from their repertoires of stories ones containing elements likely to be familiar to all participants in the correspondence, there is coherence in the sequence, linkages among messages. Some of the topical linkages that we noticed are the following: About classroom behavior, Sebastian Oscar and Anthony relate that some of the students are talking a lot in class, and

William Charlie tells about seniors coming late to class and failing to get their homework in on time. About graduation, Sebastian Oscar and Anthony name the likely graduates, William Charlie counts only 6 of 9 seniors making it, and Doug and Julie urge the remaining seniors to "get their act together." About school activities, Sebastian Oscar and Anthony tell the sad story of Tununak's loss to Toksook in the district basketball tournament, Sebastian Post tells about both the woodshop and the darkroom at school being closed, William Charlie bemoans low school spirit in Tununak, and Doug and Julie tell about Julie's doing substitute teaching in Oregon. Finally, about family, Sebastian Oscar and Anthony tell about both Sebastian's and Harry's being awarded All-Tournament pins, William Charlie tells the story of the recent adoption of Evertt, Doug and Julie tell about baby Elin calling Doug "Mom," and both the group of writers and Priscilla ask if Julie is expecting another child.

In addition to being stories linked to other stories, all of these stories are just good stories in and of themselves. There is information about time and place in which the events actually occurred (for these are reality-based stories, the favored form of story told in the village). There are well described actors and actions, and sometimes the storyteller's feelings and motivation for action are made explicit (e.g., Bobbiann and the others were shy with the new priest, the seniors are almost done with school and are goofing off). In some (the basketball tournament is a good example), there is suspense. And, in all of the stories, there is believability.

Perhaps this is what truly distinguishes the teenagers' stories: Their accounts ring so true. Whether instructive, amusing, or both, the stories can be believed—if not in every tiny detail, at least as whole tales. Even if they were imagined rather than recalled (which is apparently not the case), the events chronicled could have happened in just this way. From the stories, we learn about a life, a community. People who already know something about the life and the community (e.g., Father Delmore and Doug and Julie) would find the accounts wholly credible, but so too do those of us who know the storytellers exclusively through their stories.

## Correspondence With Other Adults

Believability is high in messages sent to other favorite adults as well. Note Hannah's telling her Aunt Bernadette of a sequence of events that Jerome Bruner (1990) would describe as both ordinary and exceptional (i.e., both washing dishes and performing in the on-the-road Yup'ik puppet show mentioned earlier):

. . . So how are Karl and Katrina doing? How'z your family doing? Our family is doing fine. Did you know my sister Leeann had a baby girl last year in march? Her baby's going to be 1 years old in march. I've been going back and forth to Toksook to go see her. The weather here is nice but very cold. I mean it's not that cold. I have about 15 minutes more till class is over. I have about 4 classes the first is Health, reading, art, and puppetry. I guess this year we'll hardly travel for the puppetry. I guess we'll try and go to GoodNews Bay that's if we can go. Our puppet shows are very short also it is very difficult to be holding the puppets up, but I'm getting used to it. it is an yup'ik puppet show. when I have to speak our language I'm always shy but I try and speak it.

Tell Karl and Katrina that I said Happy Valentines Day! I'll try and send a picture of myself when I get the time. Oh I almost forgot Uncle David and Uncle Mark are doing fine, Uncle David invited me and Shirley over to his house to go eat dinner. After eatting at this house I did his dishes when Maria Lincoln said to. . . .

Shirley also wrote to her Aunt Bernadette and again, the message is a mix of events both ordinary (babysitting, washing the dishes again) and exceptional (traveling to Fairbanks and to Anchorage)—all highly believable:

. . . Uncle David and uncle Mark are doing fine . . . , Hannah and I have been helping him., doing the dishes, and cleaning up, and I'm happy for myself. Anyways hows Katrina and Karl doing? Can you please tell them that cuz . . . Nina said "HELLO!" . . . Thank you!

During the past 4 months I've been traveling . . . I've went to Fairbanks for Search Retreat, for the very first time. And to Anchorage airport. Went over to Toksook for to baby-sit my sister Leeann's kids . . . and for the weekends. And least of all to Bethel for career days and I had a lot of fun, doing a lot of activities. . . .

Even Josh's note to President Clinton (to which there has been no response as yet, according to Hugh) is believable. Some of the students have seen on cable television that the President visits a handful of towns and cities each spring to deliver commencement addresses—why not Tununak? A letter of invitation was dispatched, and Josh is following up here:

Dear President Clinton,

Hi! How are you today? My name is Josh Kanrilak, I'm from Tununak, Alaska. Tununak is a small village by the Bering Strait. Are you coming in May? I heard you are coming here to Tununak to be our graduation guest speaker in May. I heard the 9th and 10th grader's invited you. Did you say yes? . . . I'm in the twelfth grade this year and I hope I will graduate in May. I hope you will come here to Tununak and meet us Yup'ik Eskimo people in Tununak high school. Maybe this will be your first time going to Alaska and visiting a small village. . . .

Perhaps believability in all the correspondence flows from the simple fact that Hugh encouraged the students to write honest accounts of actual events, to tell their stories. He gave them year-long opportunities to express ideas, frustrations and uncertainties. What resulted was talk between equals, in which the teenagers shared with the adults the chance to pick a topic, take a stand.

As Wayne Campbell Peck, Linda Flower, and Lorraine Higgins (1995) reminded us, adolescents often find it difficult to be heard by adults. Sometimes adults have preconceived ideas of who should legitimately control communication (usually they), and sometimes teenagers find it difficult to move from complaint and blame to description and persuasion. These difficulties did not occur in the exchanges that we have read to and from Tununak teenagers.

## DID THE STUDENTS' FLUENCY IN ENGLISH IMPROVE?

It is undeniable that the teenagers in Hugh Dyment's class have communicated a great deal this year over the Internet. They have told powerful, believable stories about events in Tununak. Their audiences, for the most part, have been adults who at one time shared a piece of village history with them—a former priest, two former teachers, adult relatives who now live elsewhere in Alaska. The exchanges with the adults are lively and coherent, representing talk between equals in which both student and adult correspondent tell stories that connect to the other person's stories. All of this is important in its own right, but we must ask if Hugh Dyment's goal of helping the students to become more fluent in their second language was achieved. Did their fluency in English improve over the course of the school year?

It seems that it did. Hugh reports that the teenagers' confidence about their own writing in English and the writing itself has improved over the course of the year. He mentions unity of expression, grammatical competence in the second language, and mechanical aspects of writing (spelling, capitalization, and punctuation) as specific areas of improvement.

As Evelyn Jacob (1995) reminded us, context is a critical element in students' academic performance. Even a slight change in context can bring improved performance. When Hugh decided not to use worksheet exercises for English grammar instruction, substituting instead actual communication with adults whom students know and like, the meaningful social context seemed to prompt the students to write, enthusiastically, for the entire year. This extended practice of writing in English, in turn, probably produced some of the improvement that Hugh observed. He describes what he observed this way:

> . . . [The Internet writing in the classroom] really does encourage and motivate students to write, however. It can be so immediate (we often send and receive responses within minutes) that my students absolutely love to write this way. . . . My students become extremely motivated then in not making grammatical and spelling mistakes. It's absolutely amazing to watch this transformation.

In the next chapters, we move away from classrooms in Alaska. We look first at a beginning teacher's Internet activity in her seventh-grade classroom in a small town in the Pacific Northwest.

# 5

# Kathy Plamondon's Seventh-Grade Classroom: Social Activity On an E-mail List

The largest and oldest trees in the world are nearly gone. The spruces, cedars, redwoods, hemlocks, and Douglas firs of the Pacific forest—some immense, many 500 years old—have been victims in what New Yorker writer Catherine Caufield (1990) has called an "orgy of logging." From the Pacific Northwest old-growth forests alone, about 3 billion board feet of timber have been produced each year since the mid-1960s. (Board feet are the measure of the amount of usable wood in a tree. One board foot is 1 square foot, 1 inch thick. It takes about 10,000 board feet of timber to build the average single-family house, and one large, old Douglas fir may contain that much timber.)

In the last decade, there have been attempts to protect a portion of the original forest of the Pacific Northwest. Environmental activists have argued that native species such as the northern spotted owl require thousands of acres of old-growth forest as habitat. Despite strong opposition from logging-industry giants Weyerhaeuser and Boise Cascade, courts have issued injunctions that have restricted logging in some areas, at least temporarily.

In this part of the Northwest, small towns and the rural areas around them are home to loggers and millworkers. The area has been dramatically affected by the injunctions, as well as by overlogging of large, old trees for 3 decades and by automation of the industry. For many reasons, the timber supply is down, and so too are the jobs available. Many loggers and millworkers are barely literate, unable to find good jobs locally when they are laid off. There are a few small farms to be worked in the area, but arable land is, in general, scarce. La Center, Washington is in this part of the Pacific Northwest.

The superintendent of the La Center school district is a conservative Christian. He and like-minded members of the small community have a strong influence on the schools in La Center. Applying a policy that is more mid-1950s than mid-1990s, the district has determined that there will be no sex education in the elementary or intermediate schools. Science teachers are permitted to mention reproduction when teaching about the systems of the human body, however, and when conservative parents object to this part—in fact, any part—of the curriculum, they often remove their children from the school and "home-school" them. The state of Washington then removes $3,500 from the general fund for each student who withdraws, so an already poor district faces further reduction of resources. The intermediate school in La Center (which includes children in Grades 5 through 8) had an enrollment of just under 400 this past year.

# LIFE IN KATHY PLAMONDON'S
# SEVENTH-GRADE CLASSROOM

Kathy Plamondon is a first-year teacher in La Center. The intermediate school in which she teaches is "departmentalized" (i.e., students move from teacher to teacher, and instead of keeping materials in their own desks, they use hallway lockers). Kathy is responsible for seventh-grade language arts and social studies instruction. Naturally, she is still learning the interactive routines of teaching—when to rephrase directions, how to explain a principle to a confused student, how much to adjust a difficult assignment, that sort of thing. Hilda Borko et al. (1992) reminded us that this is exactly what one learns in one's own classroom, not in a teacher-preparation program at the university or in a student-teaching experience in someone else's classroom. Like all teachers—even teachers in conservative districts—Kathy Plamondon has nearly absolute autonomy in her own classroom. She must solve most teaching and learning problems completely on her own.

When Tracy Kidder (1989) wrote in *Among Schoolchildren* that some of the children whom beginning teachers work with have problems that the teachers have not been prepared even to identify, let alone resolve, he could have been thinking about Kathy Plamondon's first year. No program, for instance, had prepared her to cope with the competing needs of a conservative community and a group of young adolescents just becoming sexually active and wanting to talk. Professors had talked to her about Larry Cuban's (1992) point that intellectual, emotional, and physical growth spurts make the adolescent years unpredictable ones, but no professor had told her what to do about Paula, a 6-foot tall girl, whom Kathy describes as "loud and disengaged" for much of the year. During the entire fall semester—Kathy's first semester of teaching—Paula failed to turn in any assigned work. Her mother asked not to be called about Paula, so there was no help for Kathy from that front.

On top of complex student issues, some tough resource and responsibility issues common to small, poor, mostly rural districts—the kind of districts that Jonathan Kozol (1991) described as "bleak"—plagued Kathy all year. For example, if she knew little about seventh graders when she began teaching, she knew still less about volleyball. Nevertheless, she was asked to coach volleyball, which meant 3 nights a week of practice until 6:30 p.m. and two additional nights of competition, often on the road, which kept her from planning the next day's lessons until well after 10 p.m.

And, just as human resources are scarce in La Center, so too are textbooks and other instructional materials. When a new high school was finally built a year ago, all library books in the intermediate school were moved to the new building, and a scant $15,000 was allocated to build a new collection. New almanacs and both "U" volumes of two new encyclopedia sets are already missing, but there are no funds left for replacement. Even the media specialist, who is working against great odds trying to build a usable collection and to help youngsters use it, is frustrated by a system wherein she "covers" both the high school and intermediate school and is often unavailable exactly when students are in pursuit of information and most need assistance.

In this context, in which the parents are not highly educated but have strong religious views that have curricular consequences, and in which human and material resources are lean, Kathy reports that "only a handful of students care about being successful at school." Most boasting is about stealing "chew" from the only store in town or taking the family car out for a joy ride on nearby country roads—it is almost never about academic achievement. Few of Kathy Plamondon's students aspire to college or even vocational school. Many plan to drop out after ninth grade.

What has worked best in her classroom this first year has been what she describes as "the bizarre and unusual"—letting students talk and write about Beavis and Butthead, for instance, or about Kurt Cobain. She has encouraged open, but respectful, conversation about just about anything important to her students.

Some of the talking and writing has been on the Internet. In October, Kathy Plamondon—classroom computers and connection in hand—introduced the Internet to her students, structuring their time on school computers in such a way that they rotated through a series of activities chosen by her (e.g., corresponding with Canadian pen pals, sending opinions to world leaders). A parent helper was available during part of the fall to assist students as they worked independently or in small groups. As Margaret Riel (1994) pointed out, networking experiences like this in a small, poor district such as Kathy's can help students develop interests in matters beyond the local community.

One Internet opportunity to which Kathy has introduced her seventh-grade students is KIDCAFE, an international e-mail list for 10- to 15-year-olds. Students themselves post information, read, and respond. Adults have only one role: to moderate the conversations that take place, rejecting messages that contain personal insults or that disrupt the flow of information through intimidation. Kathy Plamondon has recently taken on the responsibility of acting as assistant manager for KIDCAFE.

# KIDCAFE:
# INTERNET WRITING BY KIDS FOR KIDS

KIDCAFE participation is free. There is a single requirement: When they start out, students must prepare something called "Response to Four Questions" (Who am I? What do I want to be when I grow up? How do I want the world to be better when I grow up? What can I do now to make this happen?). Teachers are encouraged to read previously submitted responses to students, and students within a classroom are encouraged to seek help from their classmates in preparing their own responses. Messages from just three of Kathy Plamondon's students show how the same set of questions can prompt quite different responses:

> Hi, this is Jennifer. I live in a little town right out of LaCenter Washington. The name of the town is Highlands. I own and ride three horses. I have been riding since I was two years old. the town of LaCenter is very rual. I grew up on a farm & have alawys been around animals. I like Roller bladeing. Taking walks with my friends, thinking about the furture. I love going over to my Bestfriends's house her name is Bess. I am five foot six, golden brown hair and have very unusual colored eyes. Bess said they look as if there red crosses with a greenish brown back ground. . . .

Hi, this is Bess. I guess I should start with what I look like. Well I'm about 5 foot 4, I have golden brown hair. I to have unusual eye's like Jennifer's eyes, but unlike hers they have no red, they are mostly Blueish Green. I love to ride horses, but just like Evelyn we can't get horses. It's because we live in the town of LaCenter. I love dogs. Every now & then I get to go over to Jennifer's house & ride her horses. I love to play Volleyball I didn't get to play this year but next year I plan on playing. Well that's about it. . . .

My name is Nat. I live in LaCenter Washington in the U.S.A. I am 13 years old and in the seventh grade. . . .

After much thought I decided that to solve world problems we should concentrate our efforts on creating a more productive school-system. If the children had a better education then it would be easier to find the problems and solve them so it would help the economy. But many of the schools don't have the resources to fix the run down buildings or build new ones.

Schools get their money from taxes that land owners pay in their school districts. This is a problem because rural schools don't have enough land owners to pay taxes and the inner city schools have too many people living in run down low taxed buildings so they don't get very much money from taxes. When they made this law (that schools are supported by land taxes) it was a good idea because their were fewer cites and more land owners. Perhaps if we got the money from somewhere else, maybe a tax on all the students that attended the school, and spread it to all the schools that needed it and rebuild the old leaky ones. The effort to change the way kids think will take a long time and cost a lot of money but it will be worth it.

Once students have submitted their responses electronically, they are welcome to participate in the KIDCAFE List. The List is an all-day, all-night electronic conversation that operates as follows: Any kid between the ages of 10 and 15 can send a message, which moderators then check for appropriateness. The moderator sends all appropriate messages on to LISTSERV (a computer program running on a large computer in North Dakota), and LISTSERV distributes the messages to all e-mail addresses on the KIDCAFE List—many outside the United States. Participants are told that they can talk about whatever they like. Anyone on the List can respond whenever he or she chooses.

What about electronic communication of this sort would appeal to a seventh-grade student? What would account, for instance, for Paula's reaction to it? Paula, you will recall, failed to turn in a single assignment all fall. During the spring, however, she began to appear early in the morning and to stay after school, wanting to correspond on the computer. Why? We have some hunches, based on what we know about adolescents and about school and derived from reading the students' own words on KIDCAFE, archived and easily accessible to us.

## KIDCAFE Is Not Much Like School

Frank Smith (1986) wrote on many occasions about sense and nonsense in schools. It is interesting to note that most of the features of schooling that he most deplores are absent, by design, from KIDCAFE. For example, there are no grades given by moderators to students for their performance. Smith's stand on grades is a strong one: Grades stigmatize an activity as an educational ritual, worth doing only for the sake of the grade itself. Evaluating someone for fitness of function is perfectly reasonable, Smith notes, but affixing a grade to every performance is not.

There also is no coercion in KIDCAFE. Students do not need to write to other students about particular topics. They do it freely, apparently because they have something to say and a sense that other students their age might want to hear what it is. Sometimes they seek advice.

It is certainly important that there is no status differentiation comparable to what occurs in classrooms. That is, adult moderators may only moderate and, on rare occasions, reject messages containing personal insults or intimidation. They may not interrupt students, change the topic, or comment on the worth of the ideas expressed. In other words, they may not be in charge of the discourse, as they are during what Courtney Cazden (1988) called "official classroom air time" (p. 54).

## KIDCAFE Allows Discussion
## That Is Truly Interesting (to Kids)

Think about classrooms—seventh-grade world history, for instance. Philip Jackson (1990) described classroom dynamics from a teacher's perspective: Someone is asleep in the back of the room, and you can be very certain that he is detached from whatever is going on. Another student is waving his hand to indicate a willingness to give a short response to your question about

Marco Polo, and you are probably right to assume that this student is with you. What about the others? Is the student with the glassy stare contemplating an important point about trade routes or about lunch? What about the girl writing furiously? Are her notes on the spice trade or are they scribbles to a friend? Behavioral signs among students are ambiguous. A teacher's learning to be an accomplished classroom manager may ensure that he or she will see signs of attention, but it does not ensure attention itself.

Ignoring signs and thinking about actual mental states, most teachers, even first-year teachers intent on developing managerial skills, understand the progressive education maxim that students become engrossed in activities and topics in which they are interested, in which they see some connection to their most important concerns. KIDCAFE List topics—among them, wearing hats in school, gays in the military, and "dumb blonde" jokes—seem to be exactly that: initiated by kids, of high interest to kids, linked to important (kid) concerns. (Of course it is possible to allow students to write about topics of high interest to them outside the structure of KIDCAFE. As we have seen in earlier chapters, for instance, Ruth Coleman permitted students to write about topics of interest to them, and in Hugh Dyment's classroom, the students determined occasion, audience, and topic for their Internet communication.)

We have observed that concerns related to personal appearance appear frequently in the KIDCAFE archives, particularly among the girls. These concerns are powerful and memorable; well into adulthood, we remember the physical and social shortcomings that we—and especially others—noticed first during our adolescent years. Fran Lebowitz (1981) got it about right, we think:

> There is perhaps, for all concerned, no period of life so unpleasant, so unappealing, so downright unpalatable, as that of adolescence. And while pretty much everyone who comes into contact with him is disagreeably affected, certainly no one is in for a ruder shock than the actual teenager himself. Fresh from twelve straight years of uninterrupted cuteness, he is singularly unprepared to deal with the harsh consequences of inadequate personal appearance. Almost immediately upon entering the thirteenth year of life, a chubby little child becomes a big, fat girl, and a boy previously spoken of as "small for his age" finds that he is, in reality, a boy who is short. (p. 24)

## KIDCAFE Is Explicitly Social

Teenagers—in fact, people of all ages—are fascinated by other members of the species, especially by age-mates who are experiencing some of the same problems that they are. Oral and written communication, both of which are inherently interactive and social, are important ways in which humans connect with each other. As we said several pages back, Batya Friedman (1991) described telecommunications activity as *intensely* social.

Oddly enough, it seems that much inside-classroom activity can be less interactive and social than between-classroom communication with a vehicle like KIDCAFE. Linda Anderson, Nancy Brubaker, Jan Alleman-Brooks, and Gerald Duffy (1985) described classrooms in which students do seatwork, alone, for well over half of their school day. During this time, the teacher is working with a rotation of small groups of students and has assigned seatwork to keep the others occupied—sometimes profitably, often not. There is often a gap between what students know and what they need to know to complete seatwork assignments independently, and very little learning occurs in cases in which students are alone and confused, the teacher is busy, and peer assistance is not explicitly sanctioned.

When students are allowed to interact with one another, when something like KIDCAFE is available, what happens? For much of the past year, we have been reading archived messages—quite a few of them from students in Kathy Plamondon's classes. What we find are really interesting arguments, efforts by kids to persuade other kids of a particular point of view.

# ARGUMENTS ON KIDCAFE: RUDIMENTARY EFFORTS TO PERSUADE

We recently saw a *New York Times* ad for a Gerry Spence book on how to argue and win at home, in the workplace, in court. However, on reflecting on KIDCAFE arguments and other arguments made to us by children and adolescents, we are not at all certain that such a book is necessary. Children and adolescents are all argument-crafters, persuaders, as parents and teachers know only too well.

Even young children know how to offer bold assertions ("I should be able to stay up an hour later," "we should not have to form a line at dismissal time," "the library needs more books on superheroes"). Young children even know how to muster facts to support their assertions ("After all, I'm no longer a baby," "very few students run wildly down the stairs, and it looks silly to go down in a line like in elementary school," "there are mostly old books in the library, old books about real people, not about superheroes"). Fairly early in their lives, children develop at least a rudimentary ability to convince adults to act as they would like them to act.

## Structure of the Arguments

What is a little surprising to us is that the young people whose messages we read from KIDCAFE archives get their arguments so right, structurally speaking. Their arguments are not always as orderly as those philosopher Stephen Toulmin (1958) described, but, in general, they fit the model of argument parts from Toulmin. For example, they have both claims and evidence.

Claims (C) are assertions. Evidence (E) is the set of facts or examples offered in support of a claim. Marilyn Chambliss (1994) told us that competent readers have little difficulty distinguishing claims from evidence. She also reminded us that claims are invariably superordinate to evidence, as in our example:

> We should not have to form a line at dismissal time (C), because very few students run wildly down the stairs (E1), and it looks silly to go down in a line like in elementary school (E2).

(Toulmin posited a third component of arguments, *warrants,* which are links, usually implicit, between claims and evidence, but we focus in this book on claims and evidence.)

A good example of students' use of claims and evidence comes after a sixth-grade student, Tyrel, makes the following comment:

> . . . I would want to know what you think of all the pets we kill a year. I think that we shouldn't breed dogs together, unless we can take care of all the puppies.

Sharman responds to Tyrel:

> I don't like the idea of killing animals but we can't let them over populate. If we are gonna kill them it should be done in a humane way because they are living things too.

Brandon also responds:

> I agree with you, I think killing dogs is cruel. Most people just want them while they're little puppies. But when they get older they don't want them anymore so they let them loose. If anyone ever gets a puppy or dog they should keep it! . . .

Sharman has another thought on the subject, directed to Brandon:

> Brandan, yeah killing dogs is cruel. I work at a vet clinic and everyday I see at least 3 animals put to sleep. It isn't always cause the people have too it's just cause they want to. It makes me mad and I almost want to take the animals home myself. I mean if you don't want the animal why did you get it, right? . . .

We find much to praise in this short exchange. One thing is that the participants make clear, comprehensible claims about euthanizing unwanted dogs, and they provide evidence to support their claims. Another is that they operate with surprising grace considering their degree of investment in particular positions and the complexity of the topic (so, sure killing animals is bad, but what about overpopulation; maybe euthanizing in a humane manner is the answer). Also, that there is real attention, listening, to the other person's comments: Brandon introduces the idea of irresponsible pet owners, and Sharman chimes in with support in the form of personal experiences at the vet clinic.

We must remember that this exchange is a naturally occurring (unprompted) set of messages. We assume that, as with all KIDCAFE submissions, the correspondents were writing with plenty of interest in and considerable knowledge about their topic. Tyrel chose the topic and the others chose to respond, with no coercion whatsoever to join in. As Nancy Stein and Christopher Miller (1991) noted, when students are provided a topic and assigned the task of crafting an argument in school, they often have insufficient interest or knowledge (or both) to take a stand that they can support.

## Content of the Arguments

Before looking at examples of the often "hot" (controversial) content in KIDCAFE exchanges, we should note that, as Avon Crismore (1989) reminded us, language is more than content. It is also a speaker's or writer's presence in the form of words, phrases, even entire sentences that refer to the speaker's or writer's beliefs about the content—discourse about the discourse (or "metadiscourse"). Crismore gives the example of "*It is unfortunate, I think*, that women were not allowed to join guilds in the Middle Ages," in which the italicized portion of the statement is metadiscourse (disclosing the writer's beliefs about exclusion of women from guilds), and the rest is primary discourse (presenting content about the pattern of exclusion).

One would expect to find the speaker's or writer's presence in argument, especially in instances in which the person takes a strong stand and attempts to bring other participants around to that point of view. In the following exchange, in which the content is the highly controversial U.S. policy of restricting acceptance of gays in the military, the 10- to 15-year-olds use a fair amount of metadiscourse. Some of it signals attribution of ideas, some of it is qualification of certainty about ideas expressed, and some is explicit statement of personal beliefs.

Ayesha and Lisa initiate this particular discussion:

I think anyone should be accepted in the military no matter what their sexual preference. The military is not based on sexual preference but based on your performance and abilities. Homosexuals are people too the only thing that makes them different is their sexual preference! Which has nothing to with what makes up a person! How do you feel about this topic??? Keep an open mind!!!

Rachel joins in:

I personally am against the homosexual lifestyle but I am against people being restricted from jobs they feel that they could do well in.

Rob disagrees:

Im sorry but I don't think I could stand the ideas of gays in the military. I do agree that they are people and do deserve their rights, but we have to set standards for our country's national defence somewhere. Many homosexuals are very emotionaly disturbed, and I'm not sure if we need those kinds of problems

When Joyce writes, she adds some new ideas to the discussion:

I agree based on the information I know [given what follows, we assume that Joyce agrees with Ayesha and Lisa, not with Rob]. Sexual peference is a quality so is being a mother, father, brother, sister, doctor whatever!!! It is a quality not a person. Gays or Lesibians don't walk around having sex all the time or hitting on thier type, they lead a life also. Let's keep our noses out of thier bedrooms.

Laura finds a parallel between historical exclusion of Blacks and contemporary exclusion of gays and inserts metadiscourse at the end—her firm belief that her fellow correspondents can be brought around to her point of view:

I don't think that it should matter if there are gays in the militarthat gays are not alloud in the military is like saying that blacks are not alloud in the military just like it used to be. You don't want it to be like that again do you? I didn't think so.

Jody clearly disagrees with the initial point of view voiced by Ayesha and Lisa:

I think homosexuals should not be aloud in the military because what if you are bunked with a gay person and he/she comes on to you and likes you and you are straight. If they want to be that away then they should take there feelings elsewhere not where other people can be afended or hurt. Where do you think the Aids Viruse came from the gays. Thanks for reading my input and please respond!

Allen does (respond, that is):

What the heck do you mean, "If they want to be that way?" Have you ever met, talked to, or befriended a homo- or bisexual? They have no choice! It's not a lifestyle, it's a physical trait, like the color of your skin or the color of your eyes. What kind of idiot would "CHOOSE" to be gay, with all the prejudice in the world today? Furthurmore, to suggest that AIDS is the fault of homosexuals is sick, prejudiced, and stupid. No one knows for sure why the AIDS virus hit the gay community as hard as it did, but thousands (maybe more, I'm not sure) of them have died becuase of it, and you suggest it's their fault? When I was a toddler, one of my best friends was a gay person who later died of AIDS. And what backing do you have to say that any but the most perverted and sick homosexual would come on to a straight person? Is this your experience? I doubt it. I and my family have, and have had, several loose as well as good friends who were openly gay, or bisexual, and I probably have many more who aren't open about it. None of them have ever disrespected my sexual preference (hetero-sexual) by coming on to me. Don't be surprised someday if one of your good friends turns out to be homosexual.

It is interesting to note that claims presented in these messages can be clustered into two mutually exclusive clusters: support for accepting gays in the military ("Anyone should be accepted in the military no matter what their sexual preference," "I am against people being restricted from jobs they feel that they could do well in," and "Let's keep our noses out of thier bedrooms") and opposition to such a policy ("I don't think I could stand the ideas of gays in the military . . . we have to set standards for our country's national defence somewhere," and "I think homosexuals should not be aloud in the military"). There is not much middle ground here. We find much the same pattern in many of the KIDCAFE discussions: controversial topics, mutually exclusive claims, not much middle ground.

## Levels of Reasoning

Nancy Stein and Christopher Miller (1991) proposed a model for the development of argumentative skill that proves useful as we examine persuasive efforts on KIDCAFE. In general, Stein and Miller see a shift from disputative to reasoned interaction. They describe levels of reasoning used to defend a position, organized hierarchically with each successive level showing greater complexity.

At the first and most primitive level of argumentation, claims are justified solely on the basis of personal preference. At this level, one arguer says to another, "I think that $X$ should happen, because I like it" or "I do not want $Y$ to happen, because I do not like it." As Nancy Stein and Christopher Miller (1991) noted, this sort of reasoning is common at all ages. It often leads to more disputative forms of argument. There are examples of this primitive form on many topics in KIDCAFE:

> . . . It makes me mad and I almost want to take the animals home myself. . . . (Sharman, on euthanizing dogs)

> . . . I am one of the smartest people in my class. I'm sure there's alot of blond's on the board but they havta be pretty smart to know how to work a computer. I love blond jokes and I learn to take them from my friends since I am the only blond I know. . . . (Ashley, on "dumb blonde" jokes)

There are also examples of the 10- to 15-year-olds' comments crossing the fragile line from primitive reasoned to disputative interaction, and this is not surprising, for the students are still learning how to argue in a fairminded manner, learning how to pay as much attention to evidence that runs counter to their claim as they do to evidence that supports it. Also, they are usually communicating about controversial topics in which they are emotionally invested. When this occurs, tempers flare, ideas are "shouted" via CAPS (one form of emphasis on e-mail systems), and some name-calling occurs:

> . . . I am not fat and not blonde, But i STILL THINK BEFORE YOU SAY BLONDE JOKES YOU SHOULD ASK IF THAT BOTHERS ANYBOBY, . . . (Alexandra on "dumb blonde" jokes)

> Ohmigosh. I knew someone was going to come along and re-open this issue! Can't you just leave it alone?

> Anyways, I'll give you my views on this subject, since I happen to be blond. First off, "dumb blond", is just a rude stereotype. It is true that a fair share of bimbos are blond, but brunettes and red heads play a part in bimbosity also. . . . (Lindsay, "a smart blond" in the signature line, on "dumb blonde" jokes)

> . . . OK. OK. OK. I'm a boy. I think that if anyone is sexist here it is you. Yes, you bring up this OLD streotype about boys. I know about myself and about my friends: We care for sports? OK, maybe we do. Is it a problem? I don;t think so. We care for girls? What's wrong with that? I meant if boys were not interested in girls, AND VICA\VERSA, we were not here. But if you think this is all we think about? Well if you do, I'm sorry to say, but you have a serius problem. . . . (Avi, on sexism)

We are not particularly surprised that it is the topics of personal appearance and relationships (especially across genders) that seem to inflame the discourse at this level most.

At the second level of argumentation, both parties' preferences are taken into account, and the legitimacy of two (or more) claims is addressed. Counterevidence becomes important. Children and adults operating at this level understand that virtually any claim, including their own, can be challenged under certain circumstances: I acknowledge that you are right that we should not have to sit in the rain to watch the Yankees battle the Orioles, but I have seen a weather report and there is only a 30% chance of showers tonight. You acknowledge that the cable reception has been bad lately, but tonight two Woody Allen movies (our favorites!) are on. At this level of argumentation, there is a comparison of costs and benefits of pursuing each course of action. There are examples of this sort of argumentation on KIDCAFE as well:

> I don't like the idea of killing animals but we can't let them over populate. . . . (Sharman, again, on euthanizing dogs)

> . . . I do agree that they are people and do deserve their rights, but we have to set standards for our country's national defence somewhere. Many homosexuals are very emotionaly disturbed, and I'm not sure if we need those kinds of problems (Rob, on gays in the military)

> . . . And I think that maybe hats aren't allowed because of gangs, but I also think that the pricipals and superintendent's worry that the hats will be stolen from eachother, or the students may try and use there hats for a cheating object, for example writing the answers to the test on the inside of the bill, or something like that. But if the principals and superintendents, should monitor what goes on in the classes, and to ban gang slurs and colors on the hats, then I think everything should be alright, with wearing hats. (April, on wearing hats in school)

A third level of argumentation exists, and at this level, personal preferences are less important than broad social needs. General codes of behavior are invoked. An arguer is still invested in a particular position, but it is a more selfless position. Allen, who commented on gays in the military, is really the only good example of a KIDCAFE arguer (at least among the many whose messages we read) who operates regularly at this level. In his comment about gays in the military, Allen invoked a code of fairness, requiring his correspondents to acknowledge the homophobia involved in blaming gays for the AIDS epidemic, and expressing skepticism and outrage at the suggestion from another student that homosexuals routinely proposition heterosexuals:

> . . . Furthurmore, to suggest that AIDS is the fault of homosexuals is sick, prejudiced, and stupid. No one knows for sure why the AIDS virus hit the gay community as hard as it did, but thousands (maybe more, I'm not sure) of them have died becuase of it, and you suggest it's their fault? When I was a toddler, one of my best friends was a gay person who later died of AIDS. And what backing do you have to say that any but the most perverted and sick homosexual would come on to a straight person? Is this your experience? I doubt it. I and my family have, and have had, several loose as well as good friends who were openly gay, or bisexual, and I probably have many more who aren't open about it. None of them have ever disrespected my sexual preference (heterosexual) by coming on to me. . . .

To see whether Allen's skillful argumentation of relatively selfless positions held across a number of topics, we examined all messages sent on KIDCAFE between August 1994 and August 1995, searching for his. His first message was sent in March 1995, and 135 messages followed that one (Allen is a prolific communicator). Actually, his Response to Four Questions submitted in late February 1995 makes some of his views about communication explicit:

I am interested in philosophy, physics, and girls (the latter being too hard to ignore). My hobbies include computer programming and tennis. My main concern about the world is the growing divisions between various groups of people in the world. The left wing is almost completely severed from the right. The upper class has shrunk, and moved further away from the lower. There are few moderates, few middle class people. . . .

I'm fairly certain I want to go into some area of science. Maybe cosmology, maybe computer science, maybe even teaching. I'm not so much of a geek that I don't want a wife and family like everyone else, though. . . .

Mainly, I want the world to communicate. I believe that communication is the root of all consciousness. The better we communicate, the closer human race becomes to a single, living organism. . . .

Once we can truly communicate, we can far more easily solve problems such as those with the environment, and social and political structure. Fortunately, I also think a need to communicate is human nature. Many modern advancements in our culture, the establishment of the Internet itself for example, reflect this. . . .

I hope to talk and listen to more of my peers than has been possible for me for a long time. It is important that I communicate with the people who I'll be growing up with, sharing the human civilization with.

Allen, we should mention, is 14 years old. He lives in Tennessee.

For each message of Allen's that we read on a particular topic, we read at least 10 other messages immediately preceding or following his. We assessed the levels of reasoning in each message, following Stein and Miller's (1991) model. Clear contrasts in level emerged on every topic. We provide two examples.

On the topic of how well President Clinton is doing in office, a series of students evaluated Clinton very negatively. Erica's message, which we discussed before, is representative:

Hi my name is Erica. Clinton is such a dweeb. I'ts hard to believe he's a president. My dad calls him slick willy. My dad hates him thats why. Who do you want to be are president . . .

In contrast to reliance on a father's personal preference and on name-calling—primitive argumentation at best—Allen invokes two general principles of behavior (think for yourself, and evaluate Presidential performance without worrying about party affiliation):

> Wait, Erica. It's fine to agree with your dad, but it sounds to me like you're doing so just because your dad hates him. Think for yourself. Look at the things Clinton *has* done: ban quite a few assault weapons from the streets, bring economic reform, get a good jobs bill passed, and at least give a good try at health care reform. I don't want to tell you to be a Democrat, but I just think you should think about things independently from your dad.

Then, on the "hot" topic of creation theory, we see a similar pattern: primitive argumentation (including "shouting" in CAPS and name-calling) from a number of students, but reasoned invoking of general codes of behavior from Allen. John's comment clearly fits into the first category:

> Dear everybody who believes in the monkey man theory,

> Why? It's so unbelievable! Do you really think that you evolved from some apes (Who knows, maybe YOU did!)? And do you know how the idea of evolution came about? Some morons didn't like the idea of being created by God, so they invented the story that they had evolved from some apes because they found some skeletons of humans who had arthritis! Did you know that it is much more probable that a fully-functioning Boeing 747 puts itself together from junk at a junk yard after a hurricane than that humans evolved from apes during 65 billion years? Or was it 55 billion years? Oh well, ten billion years more or less doesn't matter, does it? This is no joke! Scientists figured out that that really is less probable! Also, if the Big Bang-Evolution theory is correct, than our lives just are accidents! I know my life isn't!

As does the message from Chris:

> . . . I'm not into this scientific stuff that says my Great Great Great etc. . . . Grandfather was an ape and all this crap that says that bacterial gases compounded to make a freaky fish that ate another organ that gave it legs to walk on ground and ate another one that gave it hair and after a 50 billion year cycle it was an ape that turned into a human. That's toooooooooooooooo chancy for me! I'm going with God's group

no matter what. Anything that's different I'm going to have trouble comprehending! Try reading the Bible kid! New International Version or whatever. Just make sure you understand the stuff. I'm only 13 years old, and this is probably not accurate enough, so if I wrote something wrong to other Christians than please reply. Like JoJo said "All I know is that god made me and made everything around me."

In his replies (including the one below), Allen urges KIDCAFE participants to at least attempt to understand positions other than their own. In his last lines, he commends to us something akin to what Jonathan Baron (1991) called "good thinking"—open-minded search for answers that may differ from the one that we initially favor.

. . . Very few of you take the time to actually *learn* anything about the big bang/evolution theories. No, Chris, no one has said that apes or humans evolved from "freaky" fish eating other fish that gave them legs and hair. (No one in *this* century, at least.) And no, Timothy, no one ever said that the earth had a big bang. The Big Bang created the whole Universe. Of course, even if you understood the theories of science, you may not believe them but you can't argue against someone until you at least listen to what they're saying. Chris said, "Anything different I'm going to have trouble comprehending." Yes, we all have trouble comprehending it, but just becuase it's difficult to understand doesn't mean you have to reject it without making a legitimate attempt to understand it. I won't take the time to re-explain my justification for evolution, or the scientific explanations as to how such an unlikely event as evolution happened, or rather, *must* happen. I have stated them repeatedly in my past messages. If you feel that I either haven't explained my views sufficiently, or adaquately countered the evidence you (in the plural, Creationists) have given, write—I'll write as much and as long as you want me to. But, until you read and counter *my* evidence, I don't see how to consider this a legitimate debate.

To the one or two Creationists who *have* explained themselves, and actively rejected my views: Thank you, and this message is not aimed at you.

Peace and long life,

Allen

# HOW DOES A TEACHER GET STUDENTS TO DO WHAT SHE WANTS THEM TO DO?

Kathy Plamondon has learned after one year of teaching that it is too simple to say that most kids of a certain age do not like to write. In fact, she has discovered that most seventh graders love to write at some times, and hate to write at others. Pick an index to love versus loathing, say number of words: How many words are written in response to a query on KIDCAFE (often 6 to 7 screens full) versus words written in response to an assigned topic in class? Or, number of prods needed to get writing going: How many times must Kathy Plamondon and other intermediate teachers request that students access KIDCAFE (remember Allen's 136 entries) versus the number of times that they must nudge students to begin to write a first draft? How about investment in ideas expressed: How many deep convictions supported by evidence appear in KIDCAFE arguments (that were surprisingly well structured) versus the number that appear in assigned themes that are written to be read only by the teacher? Paula's response to electronic communication, coming to school early to correspond and staying late versus her response to assigned writing, no work submitted all fall, is one clear index to love versus loathing, but not the only one that we know about.

A central question for teachers is how to get students to do what you want them to do, preferably also thinking deeply about this valued activity and actually wanting to do it. One activity that all intermediate teachers want students to engage in is oral and written communication. Kathy Plamondon and other teachers using KIDCAFE or similar electronic discussion lists seem to have found a way to get students to talk and write for months on end and to want to do so.

Surely one factor in the students' deep involvement in KIDCAFE is the social interaction involved. Seymour Papert (1980) wrote that critics of computers in classrooms worry that they might lead to less human association, to more isolation of learners. All evidence in Kathy Plamondon's class is to the contrary. In her classroom, the computer linked to KIDCAFE has become a tool for vigorous social interaction, for connections among kids across geographic (and other) boundaries.

We think that another factor accounting for deep involvement is personal control (alternatively, "self-determination" or "choice"). As we have said many times, the students, not the teachers, are in charge of the KIDCAFE discourse. They, not teachers, select occasion, audience, topic, and style of communication.

Recently, we reread Steven Goodman's (1994) story of the making of a student documentary film. It is powerful stuff, with personal control at the heart of the story. Goodman and his colleagues at the Educational Video Center spent almost a year working with four young adults (themselves products of the New York City public school system), researching, shooting, interviewing, and editing a documentary about two New York City middle-school students in two very different schools and communities: James (13, White, of Jewish and Irish descent, attending school in the middle-class Riverdale neighborhood) and Lonnie (also 13, Black, attending school in a black and Latino neighborhood plagued with massive unemployment, a thriving drug trade, and the constant threat of casual violence).

Goodman described both boys as handsome, likable, and bright. The film presents many of the images recorded textually in Jonathan Kozol's (1991) *Savage Inequalities*: Whereas, we see a clean, bright building with a well-stocked library and many academic options for James, we see noisy rooms, few band instruments, and a swimming and physical fitness instructor teaching science for Lonnie. It is not only the facts of inequity, however, that give power to the documentary project, it is also the kids' deepening understanding, as they made the film, of how race and class shape school experiences in New York City. They saw, expressed, and represented themselves, just as, in a smaller way, the KIDCAFE participants did. In both cases, it is the kids' *very words* (and visual images in the documentary) that inform and persuade.

In this chapter, we told a story about kids connecting with kids. In the next chapter, the story is about teacher connections. We meet seasoned high school teacher, Daniel Wilcox.

# 6

## Daniel Wilcox's High School Classroom: A Collegial and Public Kind of Teaching

Most seasoned teachers remember quite clearly what it was like when they began to teach, when they discovered how difficult it is. Ann Lieberman (1992), for instance, wrote that about 30 years ago she had a teaching credential from the University of California, Los Angles (UCLA), a social studies unit on Brazil in hand, and a certainty that she would work to promote active engagement with subject matter. What she found herself doing was keeping students busy, attempting to follow the curriculum, and most of all trying to survive isolation, loneliness, and a fear of losing control.

The isolation can be terrifying to a beginning teacher. There is simply no one to ask about how to unleash imagination, curb undesirable behavior, treat a crowd as a collection of interesting individuals, or make learning its own reward. Good ideas from UCLA (or wherever) dim in importance, and impulse and reaction to classroom events take their place. Even experienced teachers are apprehensive: Chris Zajac, the teacher who is the central figure in Tracy Kidder's (1989) *Among Schoolchildren,* acknowledges feeling lonely and is very concerned that often she is the only arbiter of her own professional conduct, of her success and failure with students.

Is there any hope for community among teachers? As veterans of a district-wide effort to restructure our middle school faculty into teaching teams, we are somewhat dubious about mandated restructuring to achieve community on anything resembling a grand scale. In the middle school, we found that old patterns of behavior were considerably more powerful than the new mandates: We teachers quickly pooled students at a particular grade level, but then divided them up again into traditional clumps of 25 to 30, teaching fewer subject areas and somewhat different students than before, but not really teaching very differently. We continued to plan our lessons, work with students, and assess success and failure in splendid isolation.

We are beginning to think that teacher initiated efforts on a small scale (maybe only two teachers) are preferable, and Margaret Riel (1990) seemed to agree. She argued that teachers need to use one another as educational resources, but that because they need to contend with nonstop instructional and supervisory responsibilities, they should consider computer networking as a means of connecting with one another. In Riel's plan, teachers would have computers coupled with Internet access in their classrooms. Thus, they could stay in touch with other teachers outside the classrooms with no disruption of the constant activity within the classrooms. This communication is asynchronous (i.e., it occurs in nonreal time), so teachers can receive messages while working with students and can read the stored messages at the end of the school day, replying at will.

Daniel Wilcox is a high school teacher who has just begun to use computer networking (in fact, connecting electronically with Hugh Dyment, whom we met in an earlier chapter). Hugh posted a message on AOL asking for a teacher and classroom interested in communication about work in common, and Daniel responded. Hugh tells us that "the opportunity to talk shop" with Daniel is as important to him now as providing the students an opportunity to stay in touch with other students. And Daniel, in commenting on exchanges with Hugh and other adults, added that "emailing is more like a phone call to a friend. I love it; notice how I go on and on, as if I were in a conversation." Together, the teachers have found what *New Yorker* writer John Seabrook (1995) described as private conversational space within the public space of the Internet.

Daniel is one of those teachers who arrived in a classroom after having done many other things—studying at both the University of Nebraska and California State, Long Beach; living on a kibbutz in the Middle East and managing a backpack equipment operation in California; becoming politically active; and performing community service in a Pennsylvania mental hospital for children as an alternative to entering the military. He has taught since 1982. A constant in his teaching is a love of literature, an interest in "hooking" adolescents on literature.

The high school settings in which he has taught have been as varied as his preteaching experiences. First, he worked in Salome, Arizona, a town with a population of only 350 and so remote that his wife had to drive more than 2 hours each way to stock up on groceries. When he moved to

California, Daniel taught in the farming community of Tulare and in Perris, which Daniel describes as "a rural/suburban ghetto of Riverside."

Perris may have been Daniel's most difficult assignment: A broken window in his classroom went unrepaired for 8 months, and another teacher's air conditioner failed to function properly for 2 years, with many months of temperatures above 100°. In one class, Daniel had 28 boys and 2 girls and had to refer two or three students a day for an assortment of misbehaviors. He had to break up a fight on his classroom floor one day between two girls. Still another time, squad cars were called in to stop a fight on the football field that involved more than 100 students. And yet another incident involved shots into the principal's office, apparently from an apartment building across the street. There were 11 active street gangs.

When he arrived in Santa Maria, a central coast city of about 68,000 located 10 miles from the ocean, he found less smog and a mostly agricultural area in which strawberries and a variety of vegetables are grown. It is only about 30 miles north of the huge Vandenberg Air Force Base, so many of the 12,000 Vandenberg employees live in Santa Maria. Housing is expensive, considerably more expensive than in the community near Riverside where Daniel used to live. Santa Maria is, in general, quite a contrast to Perris: very little tagging (gang graffiti) even though there are apparently two Mexican gangs and one Filipino one in town, no gunplay except for a single incident when a male student pulled a gun after school.

## LIFE IN DANIEL WILCOX'S HIGH SCHOOL CLASSROOM

Daniel describes a large portion of the population of Santa Maria as immigrants from Mexico and the Phillipines—20% or so rumored to be illegal. On the average, there are two or three White kids and one Black kid in each of his classes. (The similarity of Daniel's and Hugh Dyment's instructional settings—White teacher in an ethnic- and language-minority classroom, predominantly Latino for Daniel, exclusively Yup'ik for Hugh—surely accounts, in part, for their interest in corresponding. Daniel mentioned the similarity in one of his messages: "I'm struck by how many similarities our students have such as the fact that in both places there are many Roman Catholics and that for many, English is a second language.")

Daniel is pleased by the size of his classes (e.g., 22 students in each of two ninth-grade classes and 29 in his class of juniors, compared with 35 in one class in Perris), but he is frustrated by the large number of disengaged students in his classes, particularly the American-born students, who "are very weak academically and take little interest," who seem to believe that "value is in things, not ideas." Many of these students do not like to read. The best, most eager students tend to be the most recent arrivals in the United States. In the most recent reporting period, for instance, the highest grade among the ninth graders was earned by a student labeled both "limited English" and "migrant ed."

Daniel talks about his "foolproof interpretive poster project" as an example of low interest among the American-born students. All teachers have these activities—the ones that are successful year after year, despite dramatic differences from one year to the next in student ability, effort, and background knowledge. Every year the foolproof activity seems to engage students, and every year they seem to learn from doing it.

Daniel's interpretive poster project involves asking students to create visual arrays to represent novels that they have read or films that they have seen in the past few months. Apparently the usual submission rate is more than 95%, and work has been so good in the past that Daniel has presented the project at the Steinbeck's Teacher Seminar in Salinas. However, this year, only 65% of the second-period class submitted only moderately good posters. Daniel is openly bewildered by the difference between last year's work and this year's:

> Why the interpretive movie project failed is beyond me. I keep going over the steps to see what or why it went wrong. It was even easier this year; I didn't start it until the 3rd week. Last year, I started students on it on the second day; they hardly knew where their desks were—yet it was a resounding success, then. . . .

There are successes this year of course. Late in September, Daniel began work with his ninth graders on *Night,* Elie Wiesel's (1982) account of his life in a Nazi concentration camp. There were two obstacles to Daniel's writing to Hugh about teaching *Night* (he had to lug his computer to school for student composing and back home again for AOL access, and then, because of a hand injury, he had to type with a single finger while resting his cast near the keyboard). However, write he did. Daniel and Hugh have had a number of late-night Internet conversations about the book.

## CONVERSATIONS ABOUT *NIGHT*

Over the space of a few days of teaching and a few nights of discussion, Daniel and Hugh talked about what to teach in the book and how to teach it. Sometimes they moved from what Ellen Lagemann (1991) described as swapping shorthand accounts of "end-of-the day triumphs and complaints" (p. 2) to discussing teaching more generally. When one reads all of the messages, it is obvious that each day for these two teachers (for all teachers, surely) brings some cause for complaint. On September 29, for example, Daniel wrote:

> . . . My students had an hour and a half in the Mac Lab to write letters. They had help and a spell checker, but obviously some of them were sloppy, not even bothering to do some basic editing. I also had to censor a couple of vulgar references concerning body parts.

And, in mid-October Hugh reported that the village had been cut off from any sort of Internet access for close to 2 weeks. As if that were not frustrating enough, he could not read the pile of messages that had accumulated, because now he had to prepare to take a "senior career field trip," in which he and four seniors from Tununak would tour Anchorage, Fairbanks, Bethel, Seward, and Palmer to meet with admissions and financial aid officers at three branches of the state university and at two vocational and technical schools. Hugh describes teaching in a remote Yup'ik Eskimo village this way:

> A good village teacher, isolated by hundreds of miles from school and government bureaucrats and care givers, must fill many roles. Besides planning for and teaching academic classes (English, ESL, American History, and theater), I'm a: part-time social worker; office secretary; acting principal (4–5 school days of the month); local union representative; union bargaining team member (it's negotiation year); community/school liason; student council coadvisor; college/scholarship counselor; basketball, Yup'ik Dance festival and theater chaperone; school strategic plan committee leader; Yup'ik puppet theater director and scheduling coordinator; father confessor; editorial writer; remediation tutor; computer network cosystems operator. . . .

However, alongside complaints in both Daniel's and Hugh's messages are comments about daily pleasures and surprising causes for celebration. Daniel wrote later on September 29, for instance:

> I got a pleasant surprise—one of my 9th graders just called up asking for help with his homework. We've been discussing how short stories often revolve around a conflict. His job was to identify and describe in detail the two conflicts present in a story we've just read. . . .

And, on the same day in October that Hugh listed his roles, he also wrote back to Daniel:

> I forgot to mention in my last rant that I wouldn't give up teaching in a village right now for anything. I need variety and excitement as I bore easily. I spoke with a friend who's teaching in Bethel and decided this. The high school there is comparable to a smallish suburban school, approximately 400 students, etc. He has more security, less cross-cultural communication complications, probably a bit less stress and high achieving students. But I've got exactly what I want and need right now.

It is clear from Hugh's and Daniel's messages that neither teacher has succumbed to what Hugh Mehan (1995) called the "politics of despair," in which the old progressive agenda of actively building community and trying to make a difference in the lives of students is deemed impossible. They are both concerned about too many mandates and too few resources, but they believe that teachers are powerful, not powerless, participants in children's and adolescents' lives.

# September 26

Hugh wrote to Daniel:

> My 11th and 12th graders are reading Night. Unlike my experiences with the 9th and 10th graders and Old Man . . . it's going more slowly. I viewed Schindler's List and a Holocaust documentary with them in order to help them see and understand the book better, but they still seem a bit bored by it. Do you have any activities, writing or otherwise, that you've used that have helped the kids enjoy it?

About 2 hours later, Daniel wrote back:

> It's amazing that we are teaching some of the same books. . . . I am very surprised your 11th and 12th graders aren't captivated by [NIGHT]. I think my juniors really liked it the year I did it with them. I even think of moving it back to that age level sometimes because the historical novel I do now with juniors only works with the stronger book oriented students. It's EXODUS by Leon Uris and a great novel, but hard because of its hundreds of characters and extensive vocabulary and complicated plot. The beauty of NIGHT for me has been that remedial students can read most of the words, and yet it is so deep I

can stretch the college prep students. It's short and powerful. I've only had two or three students in the last 10 years that said they didn't like the book! I still am amazed at that, because most students won't admit they like reading even if they do. One of my former students in the past once wrote to me privately and told me he liked a certain story we had read that other guys in the class were complaining about, but then he warned me not to let the others know how he felt.

SCHINDLER'S LIST is a powerful, though I think flawed film (I'm so critical of movies). I wonder if your students were so strongly impacted by it that NIGHT seems like a repeat. At least, I think one of the reasons that my students have been so caught up with the book is that they identify with Elie and are so shocked by the almost unbelievable things that happen to him. Before we read it, I do show them a 15 minute film on the Holocaust, but they know so little about it. (In fact I often worry I don't give them enough background.)

Do you think your location or students' culture may be a factor? . . . Some things never change as I'm sure you've seen in your teaching career, but some lessons that I come to think will never fail, do. And actually, so far this year's freshmen don't seem as excited about NIGHT as students usually do; but then they didn't get wildly excited about my 'foolproof' interpretive poster either. . . .

There is more in Daniel's long reply to Hugh, but we want to interject a few comments at this point. In reading the first two messages, we are reminded of Lee Shulman's (1992) description of teaching as work that is characterized by unpredictability, uncertainty, and judgment. Daniel finds Hugh's 11th graders' interests unpredictable (his juniors really liked *Night,* but Hugh's seem considerably less engaged). He is uncertain about why the difference in response occurs: Maybe the Alaska students do like it, but won't admit it? Maybe seeing *Schindler's List* before beginning the book diminished its impact? Maybe for some reason the Yup'ik kids identify less strongly with Elie? He discusses a judgment call (that students need to be prepared, with film or extended discussion or whatever, for the book, or they will not understand it). We really appreciate the "thinking aloud" (Garner, 1987) that Daniel does, allowing Hugh to benefit from his musings (and then to respond in kind).

Another way of expressing Shulman's notion that teaching is full of unpredictability and uncertainty is Neil Postman's (1979) description of education generally as "an act of faith in the power of ideas to have consequences unforeseen and unmeasurable" (p. 230). Given this definition, Postman's advice to teachers is not surprising: Do with children and adolescents what seems rational and decent and useful to do.

Picking up on the notion of usefulness, the message from Daniel continues from the point of uncertainty about student reaction to *Night* to specific ideas about how to teach the book:

> Yes, I have some great stuff for NIGHT that I have gotten from others, plus things I've developed myself. I'll send you up some of the best, if you would like me to do that. Send me your address. One of the best things I do is a prereading motivator that I also use with other books too: The Time Chest. I got the idea from a teacher in Salinas, CA. What I do is pick up some Jewish religious articles from the local temple here in town; the rabbi has been very supportive. Each year he makes up a "goody" box for me of phylacteries, TORAH in Hebrew, prayer shawls . . . I have students come up as explorers and look at and handle the items. Then they write down what they think the articles are. . . . My wife just came to see if I'm ever quitting tonight; so just one more thing. . . .

## September 27

Daniel wrote first the next day:

> . . . Today we reached the place in the book where Elie blames God for the Nazis burning babies. (I think it is one of the most powerful sections in all of literature.) After having them write several Great Books questions in their working portfolios, I asked them to all come up and gather around on the floor inside the stage area (My room has desks in a U-shape with masking tape for a stage.) I have done Great Books for about 12 years with great success, but having seen my last sure-proof assignment—the poster project crash and burn for the first time—I was not expecting to see great discussion.
>
> Most of the students crowded up and sat on the floor, only several still in their desks, a good sign. I raised Elie's question: Why do bad things, terrible things, evil things happen to people? Then I gave them several recent examples besides the far-off one of Nazis killing babies. I mentioned the LA earthquake, the little girl killed by gang violence, and a boy that died of cancer. I reminded them of the GB rules: teacher doesn't give his answers, all answers receive credit, though teacher may press for supporting evidence. Surprise! Two hands shot up; deep thoughts were shared about why bad things happened to people.

Soon it snowballed and I had a line of hands waiting to share their thoughts on the topic. A wide variety of students . . .

It wasn't even so much that students shared; GB's almost always works for me. What amazed me was the depth of thought and the points these squirrelly 9th graders came up with and the intensity of their participation. If the bell hadn't rung, I think we could have gone for another 30 minutes without a pause.

Another factor is NIGHT. This book always seems to capture my students' concern and imagination. . . .

What caused this level of involvement? We do not think that it was the unusual seating arrangement or even Elie Wiesel's difficult question, raised again by Daniel. We think (and Daniel apparently does also) that it was mostly *Night* itself. When Barbara Tuchman (1981) discussed why historical narrative is so powerful, she said that the characters have a great advantage over purely fictional ones, in that they affect destiny: "They are significant—if not necessarily admirable. They may be evil or corrupt or mad or stupid or even stuffed shirts, but at least, by virtue of circumstance or chance or office or character, they *matter*" (p. 54).

*Night* is not only about real characters and events; it is also autobiographical. Elie Wiesel actually experienced life in a death camp and lived to write about it. We like Jerome Bruner's (1990) description of what makes autobiography a rather curious genre: "It is an account given by a narrator in the here and now about a protagonist bearing his name who existed in the there and then, the story terminating in the present when the protagonist fuses with the narrator" (p. 121).

The narrator, Jerome Bruner (1990) told us, typically recounts *and* justifies. There is a rather obvious deciding about what to make of the past at the moment of telling.

Given the content of *Night,* it strikes us as very wise of Daniel to give credit for all responses, making no right-or-wrong assessment and offering no answer to the question himself. The decision at the start of the lesson to emphasize deep thinking and broad participation (both of which then occurred), rather than recall of factual information from the book, is another example of a judgment call of the sort Lee Shulman (1992) discussed.

We do not know exactly what was said by each of the students, but we have the impression from his message that Daniel encouraged critical thinking, free expression, and open-mindedness. We know from Melinda Fine's (1993) work that, in both very obvious and subtle ways, teachers can silence students who take positions repugnant to them. A teacher's demanding clarification of arguments from just a few students and making sarcastic comments about just a few students' assertions are two tactics that Fine observed. Both undermine particular students' positions and stifle truly open discussion.

In an additional note also sent on the September 27, Daniel's only reference to *Night* was to ask, "Hugh, Where are you in NIGHT? I'm on page 33."

# September 29

Hugh's next reference to *Night* came 2 days later. He referred immediately to Daniel's comments of September 27 about the passage where Elie blames God for Nazi horrors. He wrote:

> I agree that the scene in which Eli blames God and states that he will forever more have no faith is extremely powerful. My students are 99.99% Catholic and are able to understand a people who possess a depth of faith, and are also experienced at questioning it. . . .

> Back to Night. We're on approximately page 60. We've just finished the scenes where the entire camp is forced to witness and parade before the hangings of prisoners. As was Eli, my kids were moved by the image of the young boy struggling for 30 minutes until he finally strangled. . . .

> This was following our discussion of Eli's admission that the camp is succeeding in removing his humanity as is demonstrated by his total lack of sympathy for his father during a savage beating. My kids are real clear on this as periods of starvation up here still exist in living memory, times so bad that infants and elders were the first to loose their share of what food was available. Interestingly enough, today, babies and Elders are nearly worshipped. We are all reminded daily of our responsibilities towards them.

> It appears that I was being overly sensitive when I believed that the kids weren't being made to feel anything by Night. Things are going better now but they still don't look forward to it like they would a short Steinbeck novel. . . .

> Anyway, it's late and time to hit the sack.

In reading Hugh's message, we can see the power of personal experience in understanding and interpreting text. It is seldom the case that we deal with text sentence by sentence. We frame sentences in larger structures, and we map what we are reading on to both events in our own lives and familiar stories that provide us with interpretive context. In approaching *Night,* these adolescent readers can map what Elie experienced on to their having been alone and having felt afraid, and in so doing, they can understand, if only in part, how Elie must have felt. Both Daniel and Hugh assist in this process: Daniel mentions an earthquake and gang violence close to home, and Hugh builds on the community memory of starvation in the village.

Of course, part of the power of *Night* is its blend of the truly exceptional (the events that occur in the camp) and the very ordinary (the characters, who remind us of noble people in our own lives). As Jerome Bruner (1990) pointed out, when we encounter an exception to the ordinary and the expected (e.g., the horrors in the camp) and when we ask why this thing occurred, we are often told stories. That is what Elie Wiesel has done—attempted to give meaning, some explanation, to truly extraordinary, horrible events. A story, Jerome Bruner tells us, is supposed to make deviations from the ordinary at least partly comprehensible.

## October 2

The following Monday, Daniel wrote again:

> . . . We finished the oral reading of NIGHT today. My first period were with it all the way. But I wish I would have broken up the reading for my second; some of them drifted on me during the last 15 minutes, and so I don't think they finished feeling as strongly impacted. Oh, well, I will be less hurried next time.

> I passed around an actual picture of Eli taken in the concentration camp when he was liberated, showing himself as he describes himself on the last page. Then I passed around a picture of him from the present. He was also just in the local paper, but I couldn't find my copy. Because of the restrictions of my casted arm, my files are disorganized and in a clutter.

> Sometimes I show them a video of an interview with Eli, but I am going to skip it this time because it is slow. Instead, I am launching them right into their NIGHT project after they do a worksheet on the values of the main characters.

Why oral reading, especially if some (or most) of the reading is by the teacher? Hugh wrote early in the correspondence with Daniel that he reads aloud, sometimes alternating between a page that he reads and one that a student reads, so that listeners can generate images of characters and events and so that the story moves forward. Reading the book silently, page after page, can be difficult going for students for whom English is their second language (L2). It is a short book, but much of the vocabulary is new, and motivations of characters are complex. Catherine Snow (1992) noted that some challenging literacy tasks take years for L2 learners to master. She added that L2 skill in listening often differs dramatically from L2 reading skill.

## October 4

In the final exchange about *Night* that we present in this section, Daniel sent some of his students' "5-minute responses" on to Hugh. Daniel had prompted the responses in the following manner:

> On a scale of 1 to 10, 10 being the best, how would you rate NIGHT? Explain why you gave the rating that you did. Then write two interpretive questions about the book for which you don't have answers. The harder the question, the better. If I can't answer the question, then you will get extra credit.

There is little ambiguity in this grading plan: Questions with many possible answers (e.g., "Why did the Nazis imprison the Jews and make them do work, rather than just killing them right away?") are valued more than questions with only a single correct answer (e.g., "Who played music in the book?"). The students provided high ratings and complex, thoughtful questions.

# CONVERSATIONS
# BETWEEN INTERESTING ADULTS

In the midst of reading the conversations between Hugh and Daniel, we began Deborah Meier's (1995) book *The Power of Their Ideas,* a book filled with ideas that emerged from Meier's founding and continuing to work in a small East Harlem school called Central Park East (CPE). Meier was one of six teachers—three White, two Black, and one Latino—who opened the doors to about 100 children in kindergarten through third grade in 1974. Most of the children were Black and Latino, most poor. CPE has since grown from one school to four, and it now enrolls students from kindergarten through high school.

The six teachers who were there at the start had in common a concern about low and trivial expectations and discrete-skill approaches found in many urban public schools. They also shared a strong desire to put resources at CPE into classrooms, not into bureaucracies (an answering machine served as the initial administrative office.) Deborah Meier (1995) wrote about the group's desire for greater autonomy as teachers:

> We spoke a lot about democracy, but we were also just plain sick and tired of having to waste so much time and energy negotiating with school officials over what seemed like commonsense requests, worrying about myriad rules and regulations, being forced to compromise on so many of our beliefs. We came together with our own visions of what teaching could be if only *we* had control. We saw parents as crucial, but viewed their input as advisory. (p. 23)

It struck us that this same desire for greater autonomy in making decisions about curriculum and teaching appears in many of Hugh's and Daniel's exchanges. In an early message, Hugh wrote about teaching style:

> . . . I'm finding that such a small number of kids really allows me to be a "sage on a stage. . . ." I know that this type of delivery is frowned upon by many educational researchers, and by some liberal reformers, but I find it effective if used out of concern.

The next day's message from Daniel included a comment on current curricular emphases in California high schools:

> . . . The big push here is in school to job, career paths, and I'm not against students finding a career early and improving their lot in life. I certainly wouldn't want them to follow in my footsteps, careening around the world for 10 years after high school. But having students select paths before they have even asked the great questions seems to be one of the weaknesses of current educational mania; it just sucks 9th graders into the lie that money and job is all.

A few days later, Daniel wrote again, this time expressing strong views about the teaching of literature:

. . . This shows where personal experience weighs more in how a teacher teaches than his educational readings. I always wanted long and detailed comments on my papers and so think I need to give them to my students. . . . As I look back on all the top-down changes in education that have been loaded on me in the last 15 years, the vast majority of it has been chaff. Students have learned best when I introduced a work of literature that I loved. . . .

And, shortly after that, Hugh wrote a long note on his educational philosophy, in which he made the following points about learning to teach and teaching:

. . . Public school districts are top heavy with management, are encumbered with red tape and are regulated to death. . . .

And:

. . . My kids usually only catch fire when I am teaching something I love. This happens most often with literature and world history. The specific teaching method I use doesn't matter much when they know this is exciting. When their eccentric teacher is visibly enthralled by something they get cranking and they learn . . .

And also:

. . . I truly don't believe that [learning occurs] because I've mastered some teaching technique or learning theory. . . .

And finally:

. . . Eight years ago, when I was 24, I applied for an innovative Education masters and certificate program that the Maine university system was experimenting with. Basically, course work was at least equalled by time spent in the classroom with a master teacher. I wasn't accepted and I shouldn't have been accepted. My personal life was a shambles and I wouldn't have been capable of really achieving much at that point. However, I firmly believe that I wasn't accepted for the wrong reasons. . . . I stated many of the things I've stated here but this didn't sit well with university instructors who's careers were designed around teaching people how to teach. Of course stating these things when I had zero teaching experience under my belt weakened my argument. . . .

Readers of this book might ask why Hugh and Daniel so openly expressed their belief in the wisdom of practice—and the folly of listening too carefully to an assortment of nonteaching "others" (e.g., researchers, reformers, teacher educators, administrators, and writers). After all, the teachers know that we who read each of their messages no longer teach in public school classrooms, and they also know that as educational researchers, teacher educators, department chair and technology center directors, and writers of cases we fit rather neatly into their "others" category. The apparent candor in their messages implies to us that either they forgot after each long day that we are routinely copied in their messages (in this explanation, we are like videotape cameras running after a few days in the backs of classrooms) or—this is the explanation that we prefer—it is the case that all of us have established a certain amount of trust.

Trust is another topic in Deborah Meier's (1995) book. She wrote that we all acknowledge that 5-year-olds learn best when they feel relatively safe, physically and psychologically. Surely this is so for older students and teachers as well, she suggests. Part of feeling safe, in Meier's view, is trusting at least some of those "in charge," not to mention being able to predict with some degree of accuracy how the place operates. So, if "the place" is school, Hugh and Daniel must have some degree of certainty that at least some administrators expect them to behave with some amount of autonomy in their classrooms. And, if "the place" is this book, Hugh and Daniel must have believed us when we told them that we were sympathetic witnesses to their practice.

The main reason why we mention Deborah Meier, however, is not to discuss teacher autonomy or trust. Instead, it is to emphasize the importance of conversations between interesting adults who happen to be teachers. As we said at the start of this chapter, teachers have to survive isolation and loneliness. One way to survive is for every interesting adult to seize each available opportunity to talk to other interesting adults who are interested in, among other things, kids and teaching, who are interested enough to think, read, and even write on occasion about them. This survival plan seems to us to be a sound one for teachers of mathematics and science as well as for teachers of literature and history. The need for conversation and the benefits of being collegial and public about practice are not limited to teachers of any particular subject matter or age group.

Meier says that teachers need opportunities to speak and write about their work. After all, she adds, human beings are by nature social, interactive learners who see how others do something (e.g., engage high school students in *Night*) and then see if it works for them. We noted in the introductory chapter that telecommunications is intensely social activity, an opportunity for children to learn from other children, crossing cultural, economic, and regional borders while they do so.

The same point can be made for teachers, who, in the best of all possible worlds, try daily, just as children do, to make sense of their world and to learn. In this best of all possible worlds, teachers would do what Penelope Peterson (1994) advised both educational researchers and teachers to do: Make your "invisible" beliefs about subject matter and about teaching and learning explicit. Then, openly admit when you have revised your thinking.

Meier (1995) also pointed out that few policymakers understand what it means to teach a student year after year following someone else's design. Teachers do though, and they also understand why they and their colleagues can be prickly and defensive about their work in classrooms: After all, this is work that involves making life-altering decisions daily (e.g., calling on children when they are most, not least, likely to know; intervening in a dispute only to prevent emotional or physical harm, not to obstruct independent problem solving).

Wise teachers form what William Ayers (1993) called "lifesaving" alliances (p. 131), engaging each other in conversations about practice. They provide something to each other that no one else can give: abundant examples of really terrific ideas and of truly awful ones, examples of activities that stand a chance of unleashing creative, thoughtful response and of those that seem doomed to produce snores or parroted nonsense. In fact, teachers probably learn most when hearing from each other about what Meier (1995) labels "near-misses, almosts, and downright failures" (p. 179).

When we finish eavesdropping on Hugh and Daniel, we intend to suggest that they read Deborah Meier's (1995) book. After all, both by word and deed, they have demonstrated that they wholly understand and support what she says about learning: "There are, in the end, only two main ways human beings learn: by observing others (directly or vicariously) and by trying things out for themselves. Novices learn from experts and from experience. That's all there is to it" (p. 181).

The first message that we read in the Hugh–Daniel correspondence consisted of Hugh's asking Daniel for help in getting his students involved in *Night*. A recent message completes the circle. It is Daniel's asking Hugh for assistance with telecommunications in the classroom. He writes:

> As I am just getting into telecommunications in the classroom, I am curious about how others got started and the methods they use. For instance, I would like to know as much as you have time to share about your setup, computer, layout of classroom, relationship of email to rest of assignments and grades, etc. . . .

The work of teaching children and adolescents is profoundly important and, luckily for all of us, some very interesting people choose to engage in this work. They can learn from each other. Internet conversations of the sort that Daniel and Hugh have had help them do their work just a little bit better.

In the next chapter, we meet another interesting person who teaches children. Kathy Nell and her fourth-grade students have discovered the World Wide Web. They use the Web to share work and to communicate with other classrooms around the globe.

# 7

## Kathy Nell's Fourth-Grade Classroom: Literature and Social Studies Activities on the Web

Adept teachers have both a deep knowledge of the subject matters they teach and a rich set of understandings and beliefs about how to teach. What is less obvious sometimes is that they also have knowledge about the *teachability* of particular subject matter, such as history or literature—knowledge about the most powerful analogies, demonstrations, and examples for the topics that they most regularly teach. They have figured out how to tailor content, how to make a particular subject comprehensible to students. Lee Shulman (1986) called this knowledge about teachability and tailoring "pedagogical content knowledge."

Take history. Suzanne Wilson (1992) provided the example of an American history teacher deciding how to explain the relations between England and its North American colonies. The teacher might use a mother–child analogy, Wilson suggests, because it is reasonable to assume that students know quite a bit about the parent–child relationship and can use this knowledge to develop understanding about England and its colonies. In fact, the analogy was used in the colonial world to explain the role of the colonies with respect to the "mother country."

Another example from history involves demonstrating to students how to use corroborative detail, which Barbara Tuchman (1981, p. 34) called "the great corrective" to bias in documents. High school students could be helped to read and interpret entries from 1936 in a pro-Franklin Delano Roosevelt campaign worker's diary, newspaper accounts of the "campaign train" from tiny mining towns like Thomas, WV, and perhaps telegrams

**107**

flowing between the reelection team aboard the train and the White House. They could check back and forth among the documents for overlap and contradictions, trying to sort out what happened in this phase of the Presidential election of 1932 and why.

As for literature, Linda Levine (1993) provided us with an example from a K–1 room of culturally and economically diverse East Harlem students. The teacher in the classroom had initiated a daily routine called "reading time," in which, for 20 minutes or so at the start of each morning, every child worked with books, some reading, some using pictures to "read" a story. By December, the children's confidence was such that the teacher began "reading with the group," in which an individual student sat in the teacher's chair and shared a story (interpreting pictures or print) with the rest of the class. Before sharing, each child had a private discussion with the teacher about the book to be shared, and after sharing, the child fielded questions from the rest of the class. The sessions were not wholly conflict-free. The students frequently argued about the truth of a particular story.

The teacher could have taught the children an important lesson about literature by telling them outright that narratives must be interpreted, that they can be interpreted in different ways by different readers (Bruner's, 1990, point, which we discussed in chapter 3). However, the teacher chose to teach this point by example. When young Martin (a picture interpreter) shared *The Gingerbread Man*, and told his audience that the Gingerbread Man had drowned, he was attacked by another student, Charlie, who insisted that the fox had eaten the Gingerbread Man. The teacher chose this moment to tell the class "Look. Look at the picture. All we see here is the fox in the water alone. There are different ways to understand this picture, different ways to read the story."

Kathy Nell is a teacher who has considerable pedagogical content knowledge, acquired in part from teaching 3- and 4-year-olds, then second and fourth graders, for 23 years in the Philadelphia school system. Sigrun Gudmundsdottir (1995) told us that experience (trying things out, observing, talking to other teachers) is the usual source of practical ways of knowing subject matter.

Kathy and her current fourth-grade students in room 308 at Edwin Forrest Elementary School in Philadelphia have discovered the World Wide Web (WWW or Web), a large-scale hypermedia network (i.e., a learner-driven system that allows someone to navigate through information in a variety of formats). The WWW has text, pictures, moving images, and even audioclips, and Kathy and her students use all of them. They use them to share their work in particular subjects, and they use them to communicate with students in other classrooms.

# LIFE IN KATHY NELL'S
# FOURTH-GRADE CLASSROOM

Many large urban school districts, Philadelphia among them, have sought money from the U.S. Department of Education in the last few years in order to outfit their K–12 classrooms with computers and online access. The need is there: Earlier in this book, we noted that 1995 National Center for Education Statistics data show that even though 75% of public schools have computers with some type of telecommunications capability, only 35% have access to the Internet. More secondary schools have access than elementary schools, and larger schools (with enrollments of 1,000 or more) are about twice as likely as small schools (with enrollments of less than 300) to have access.

In many urban districts, where decrepit buildings, high truancy, and low test scores are common, telecommunications readiness becomes an equity issue. Teachers and students in classrooms with scarce resources can access information and human resources beyond the walls of their classrooms if computers and online access are made available.

Philadelphia has fared well in resource-seeking, receiving a large grant to buy equipment later this year and in years to come. However, for the present, Kathy's work on the WWW is well in advance of significant support from the district, and she has spent a great deal of her own money. Apparently, this is not unusual: Lynne Schrum (1995) reported that most teachers have to fight for limited resources and are usually expected to "dig deeply into their own pockets" (p. 227). Kathy has two computers in her classroom, one that she owns and one that she received from a grant. One modem in the room is hers, and one is from the grant.

The WWW work in Kathy's classroom usually goes something like this: The students' written work, whatever the subject, is done at the computer, with the children doing all their own keyboarding. When work is edited (by authors and by peer editors) and ready to be shared, Kathy prepares it for the Web pages, working with a district person who actually puts the work on the Web. Scanning of Halloween art was done by Kathy's nephew at his house.

Communication is an important part of all this work. Kathy has inserted envelope icons throughout the Web pages as general prompts to readers ("Class 308 would love to hear from you") and she has also put them next to each piece of student work, so that messages can reach individual authors. This works in the following manner: A reader in another classroom (or wherever) selects the envelope icon near the piece of work, opening an Internet mail window into which a message can be typed and then sent. (They are cautioned to put the student author's name on the message, as there is only one mailbox for the entire class.) Students in Kathy's classroom check their own mail and answer it. Kathy reports that it takes many hours each day for all the children to do work and send and receive mail at only two computers, but interest is high ("[Students] love to get mail addressed to them," she says). Children come to school early and choose to work at lunch and during recess time.

## AN ASIDE: A LITTLE MORE INFORMATION ON THE WWW

Because Kathy and her students browse and publish there, it seems important to provide a little background information on the Web. As we said earlier, it is a *hypermedia system,* which means that from any document in any format (a poem, a story, a short greeting like the following two), you can get to more information:

> Hello, my name is John C. I live in Pennsylvania, U.S.A. My favorite food is chicken. I'm aggressive, I like <u>Hockey</u> and Lacrosse. I like to read Goosebumps, and my favorite is Something Wicked Comes This Way. I'm a blue belt in karate and my favorite wrestler is Diesel.

> Hi I'm Joseph S. I'm in the 4th grade. I am 9. I eat pizza. I like math alot. I make models. I like the color black. I like Ronin Warriors. My favorite book is the Mask. My idea of a perfect day is going across the Caribbean. I'm a boy. Twenty years from now I will be a <u>astronaut</u>.

Kathy and her students marked places where more information can be accessed (e.g., "Hockey," "astronaut" in these messages). On the screen, these places are highlighted. When a reader selects one of these places (a *link*), and "clicks" on it, other information on the Web is accessed. In the case of "Hockey," a National Hockey League home page appears, and in the case of "astronaut," a NASA home page appears. (A *home page* is a title and table of contents for a Web site.) Additional information can appear in the form of text, images, sound, animation, or some combination of these. The process of moving from a document to background information is rather like using an electronic footnote system, except that in this case, the system capitalizes on text plus other media.

The fact that the WWW is a learner-driven system is both an enormous strength and a potential problem. The strength of the system is obvious when learners seek specific information and use documents linked to other documents to find it—not unlike an adept library user running from one part of a vast collection to another in search of information, but at a considerably faster pace. The problem is that, as we noted in Gillingham, Young, and Kulikowich (1994), users can get lost in hyperspace, intrigued by a detail here and an image there, forgetting their original goals. A scenario of a group of students who are somewhat mindlessly clicking on links deeper and deeper into background material (i.e., more distant from the original entry point) is usually not quite what teachers have in mind when they decide to use the WWW as a classroom resource.

The WWW is flourishing. As John Markoff (1995) wrote in *The New York Times,* the Web (like the Internet) was little more than a research tool for physicists and computer hobbyists only 3 years ago, and today it is embraced by businesses and media concerns alike (the Associated Press adopted the medium just this fall as a means of distributing its articles and photographs over the Internet). The big breakthrough came in 1992 when student researchers at the National Center for Supercomputing Applications in Illinois created Mosaic, a software tool that is called a *Web browser.* With Mosaic, users could access information anywhere on the WWW by pointing and clicking a computer mouse on highlighted words or images on the screen (like "Hockey" and "astronaut" in Kathy's students' messages).

Thousands of Web sites are created each month. It requires little money and only moderate computer skills. In the *Times* article, Markoff (1995) makes the interesting point that, at least at this time, the Web serves a complementary role to other print and electronic media: Many radio stations and all major television networks have Web sites promoting their programs, and many newspapers, including the *Times,* are devising Web editions.

# PERSONAL RESPONSES TO LITERATURE ON THE WEB

Literature-based instruction occurs in many elementary classrooms today. What is it? Kathryn Au, Jana Mason, and Judith Scheu (1995) provided a brief description that we like: Children read and write about books that meet high literary and artistic standards—entire books, not excerpts from them. This sort of teaching requires of teachers that they are clear about the literacy knowledge, skills, and dispositions that they want children to develop—and that they are very familiar with many books. As Kathy Nell puts it, "I have so much curriculum in my head that at times I feel as if my head is about to explode with ideas."

A reader's personal response to literature is central in literature-based instruction. Students are often asked to discuss or write about their feelings about novels and about connections between the novels and their own lives. Teachers who support literature-based instruction have in common a belief that children's and adolescent literature can provoke amusement, fear, sadness—in fact, a full range of aesthetic responses.

They also believe that they should respect students' perspectives, but offer additional interpretations of literature that may not have occurred to the students. Think of Levine's example of the K–1 children in East Harlem interpreting pictures in *The Gingerbread Man* and of Daniel Wilcox's high school students grappling with Elie Wiesel's (1982) question about evil in *Night* (see chap. 6). Both groups of students (at very different ages) were learning that literature is open to more than one interpretation.

Students in Kathy Nell's classroom read many pieces of literature representing many genres. Kathy often selects historical fiction that links to social studies work in the classroom and modern fiction that links to her students' real-life experiences. Gloria Ladson-Billings (1994, p. 117) emphasized how important it is to bring "the culture and everyday experiences of the students" into literacy learning, and modern fiction that touches on themes important to children (e.g., loneliness, envy, urban violence) can be an especially useful vehicle for this.

# Poetry

One genre that Kathy's students read and write about is poetry. Poetry, more than perhaps any other genre, uses very few words to convey multiple images and sounds. Poetry is often read aloud in Kathy's class, often used as a stimulus for the children's own writing. In the Fall, to accompany the poems that were composed, the class produced photographs of the poets. Both poem and photo then appeared, side-by-side, on the Web.

To produce the photos, they experimented with a new computer tool called QuickCam, a black-and-white camera that costs about $100. The camera plugs into a computer through the modem or printer port and is, according to Kathy, very easy to use. Classes can produce either still photos or QuickTime movies.

Kathy's attention to authorship strikes us as being very important. When she and her students encourage readers in distant classrooms to write to authors by selecting the envelope icon near individual pieces of work and when they feature photographs of poets, Kathy supports the notion that the children's writing is far more than transcribed or paraphrased writing from someone else: It is the highly individual ideas in one's head moved to the printed page (or, in this case, to the computer screen). As we said elsewhere (Garner & Alexander, 1994), literature—in fact, all text—is authored, written in a time and place for a particular reason. Kathy's emphasis on authorship makes this point clear to her students.

Kathy has recently made this point still more clearly. She has generated "electronic portfolios" for each student in her class. Now, if a distant correspondent wants to see all of a particular student's poetry (or other work), the person can access the work plus pictures and an audio clip from the student just by clicking on the student's name.

Here are just four of the poems written by the children this fall (remember that a picture of each poet also appeared on the Web):

Sometimes
Hi my name is Brian
sometimes my mind goes flying.
sometimes I wonder what I'm gonna be
sometimes I wonder what I'm gonna do
sometimes sometimes sometimes
sometimes I wish I knew
Kung Do you? I do
sometimes sometimes sometimes.

Gotta Rap by Hassian K.
want to rap to my mouth
turns dry and I can rap all
day going to and coming from
schools feels so good today
feels so good on a rainy
day I remember when I rap
to my cousin on the phone want
to rap want to rap so
bad about my name is
Hassian and I like to
get down on the dance floor
and rap and rap
and I'm
going nuts

The First Time by Corey S.
The first time I rode my bike
it was fun
the first time my dad
took me fishing
I caught a trout
the first time I learned
how to read
it was hard
the first time I rode
a horse
it was fun
the first day
at school was scary
the first time I learned how to multiply
it was very hard

Nine by Alexis M.
Nine is a cool age.
Nine is my friend's age.
Nine is a fine number.
Nine is my sister's
favorite number.
I like being nine.
You can use the number nine in math problems.
My mom uses it in her typewriting.
But my dad does not like the number nine.
He likes the number ten.

## Stories

Some of the highly individual ideas that students in Kathy Nell's class move to the computer screen appear as stories, full of energy and based on the children's personal experiences. Most of them would be characterized by Shirley Brice Heath (1983) as "true stories," much like those from Tununak (see chap. 3)—based on real events, with only slight exaggeration of action and outcome.

Kathy prompted the stories by asking, "What was your proudest, happiest, saddest, weirdest, silliest, most serious, scariest, funniest, most important, or most embarrassing moment of your life?" For each published story, a title, an author's name, and the envelope icon appear. In addition, distant readers are encouraged to send their own stories to Forrest Elementary: " . . . Please send us copies of your stories. We would love to read them."

A real benefit to being a Web-active classroom is that a teacher can introduce the notion of revision for a distant audience. Not everything needs to be moved beyond first draft stage, but when students want to produce a publishable piece, they have to be certain that they have made their work interesting, paid attention to flow of ideas, and cleaned up mechanical errors. Revising for publication is a way of life for professional writers and academics, and it can become an important part of fourth-grade life as well. Teachers often prod students to revise "for a better grade," but the goal of revising for publication to a distant audience is much to be preferred, we (and Kathy) think.

Revision works something like this in Kathy classroom: Children compose the initial draft on paper or at one of the two computers. Even though "editing is something that they take as a personal criticism of what they have written. . . . Some kids still think that editing means starting all over everytime. It is a hard concept for fourth graders to understand," Kathy tells us that many editing cycles follow composing and precede publishing: self-editing, peer editing, teacher assistance, use of a spell check on the word processor, and sometimes a read-aloud to children who have completed their own work.

Here are just some of the stories, revised for publication:

My Weird Face by Theresa F.
Once I was sleeping in my bed. My dad walked into my room to turn off my light. My dad saw me sitting up in my bed. I was smiling in my bed. My dad asked me if I was all right and I said yes. My dad told my mom about my face and she laughed. The next morning my dad told me about my face. I laughed. My dad told my brother about my face and he laughed. When my dad showed me what my face looked like I laughed so hard tears came out of my eyes. My face looked very weird. The next day I told my friends about my weird face. They all laughed when I told them the story. They kept on asking me to tell them the story over again. Every time I told them the story they laughed.

The Proudest Day by Kenneth M.
My proudest day was when I went to the baseball championships. I felt very happy. My mom and dad were there and my two brothers were also there. The team I was playing was Crispen Green. We were

winning. We were up to bat. It was my friend Jimmy's turn. He hit a home run and we won the baseball championship. It was the proudest day of my life. We got our baseball championship trophies. When we got to the club house we poured a cooler of water on my coaches head.

My Scary and Funny Day by Andrew S.
It all happened on August 21, 1994. My dad, my cousin and I went crabbing in a big red boat. It was hard to catch the crabs but I caught three at the same time. My dad caught ten but he was out longer and my cousins crab got away. Then we were heading home and I accidentally knocked over the bucket of crabs. There were no seats to jump on. I tried to sit down but a crab bit me. My dad jumped in the water and the boat tipped over and the crabs fell. My cousin and I jumped on the back of the boat. My dad unhooked the paddles and we had to paddle our way back. Luckily we didn't go out far. We made it back. What a day!

My First Trophy by Brian B.
When the judges were picking people for the karate tournament. I was nervous. My grandpop drove me that day. My mom was there too. As soon as I got there I had to fight. I was scared because I had to fight a ten year old and I was only six. I lost. I was so mad. I asked the referee if I could fight again. He said I could. I thanked him. I told the boy we were going to fight again. He laughed. I got even madder. The referee told us to start. The boy did not hear him. I did. I kicked him in his legs and he fell and I pinned him. I was so happy. That's how I got my first trophy. I came in third place.

My Funniest Day by Corey S.
The funniest day of my life was at my ninth birthday. My cousin was there. He pushed my head into the cake and I pushed his head into the cake. We got cleaned up and we went to the park. We had a lot of fun with my new football. When we went back home we played Sega and then we went for pizza at Chucky Cheese. We played a lot of games. I won five hundred tickets and I got a lot of prizes. I played more games and got more tickets. Then we went home and went to bed. My cousin went home and he said he had a lot of fun.

Megan was perhaps luckiest of all. Just after her story "My Dog Died" was published on the Web, she received messages from two college-age readers, Kristi and Wally. Each expressed a personal response to Megan's story: Kristi too lost a dog, and Wally has a dog named Max, just like Megan did. Here is the story that prompted Kristi and Wally to write:

My Dog Died by Megan H.

One of the saddest days of my life was when my dog Max was sick. He was sick for three days in a row. It was really rough. My dog was sick because he swallowed a big bone. He was a rottweiler and every body loved him. He started throwing up. We took him to the veterinarian. The vet people said he would be fine. He was still sick though. I got scared and sad. A few hours later he had a seizure right on the floor of the house. My dad's girlfriend called the animal hospital and we put Max in the Jeep. She took him to the veterinarian again. A friend stayed with us. She called my dad and told him all the information he needed. Then she took us home. I told my mom what had happened and she said it would be all right. I fell asleep. The next day at school I was scared. After school my dad picked me up. I asked him how Max was doing. He said that Max did not make it. He said at first he did but then he drank some anti-freeze when he got home and died. I cried. My dad said we would get a new dog. I thought we would have Max for a long time. I hope the new dog we get looks just like Max.

# DEVELOPING EMPATHY THROUGH SOCIAL STUDIES ACTIVITIES ON THE WEB

In thinking about Kathy Nell's social studies program, we found Fred Newmann's (1991) discussion of "the intellectual terrain" of social studies useful. Newmann identifies five big ideas that are part of the terrain—each bigger than individual concepts, explanations, or issues. One of the ideas is empathy, which is important to Kathy and essential to McLuhan's (1964) notion of the global village.

Fred Newmann (1991) defined empathy as the expansion of students' social experience across time, space, and culture, going beyond the familiar to the unfamiliar and attempting to incorporate the experience of others into one's own thinking. Needless to say, empathy is more readily achieved in classrooms in which there is sustained examination of a few topics, rather than superficial coverage of many. Kathy Nell is open to the principle of in-depth inquiry on a few topics.

## Participating in Sister Cities Online

Kathy has used a Scholastic Network idea since school began this fall. Her students are collaborating on a number of projects with students in a fourth-grade class in Dinuba, CA, near Fresno. The November activity, just completed, required the Forrest Elementary School students to list "signs of the season" where they live and to request that the children in California do the same. This is part of going beyond the familiar to the unfamiliar, seeing similarity in the experiences of distant peers—and difference.

The children in Kathy's class divided into groups to make lists, the class picked the best ideas, and each student played a role in typing ideas at the computer to send off to California. One student typed the introductory notes. Note that Lines 6, 15, 19, 20, and 22 are likely to be more familiar to children in the Northeast than in California and that Line 21 is surely more familiar to children in urban areas than to children in small towns:

Dear Roosevelt School,

Hi, how are you? These are the things that we noticed about the seasons, and we're suppse to get some snow tonight. It is raining here today and the wind is very strong. They call it a Nor'Easter storm when it comes up the coast. In the summer is sometimes brings a hurricane. We are suppose to get about 2 inches of rain today.

Signs of the Seasons in Philly:

1. Leaves are rotting
2. Birds fly south because it's warm in the south
3. Football season starts
4. Days get shorter
5. Pick up dead flowers
6. Frost grows on the windows at night
7. We rake the leaves
8. We bring plants in
9. Base Ball season ends
10. We drink hot choclate
11. We eat hot food
12. We buy warmer clothes
13. The wind gets heavy
14. Squirrels get lots of nuts
15. We turn on the heaters
16. Warm pjs and warm kisses and warm blankets and pillows.
17. The leaves fall down and scatter on the streets.
18. Basketball and Hockey starts.
19. In the winter we knock on people's doors and ask them if we can shovel snow to get money
20. You put a cover over the bushes for the frost.

21. The homeless people sleep over the heaters on the sidewalks in our city.
22. You can go ice-skating.
23. We buy mittens, boots and winter coats.
24. We put all our summer clothes away for the winter.

Happy Thanksgiving to you guys.

Sure enough, the list that came back from California was quite different (note, especially, Lines 2, 6, 7, 8, 9, 11, 14, and 15):

Dear Forrest School,

. . . These are the things that we noticed about our seasonal change. We usually have rain by now. However, it hasn't rained yet. We only have an average of about 7 inches of precipitation here in Dinuba, California.

1. We are still doing outdoor activities.
2. People don't use their pool anymore unless they are heated.
3. We rake up leaves for money.
4. Thanksgiving is coming soon.
5. The flu season is here.
6. We are still wearing short sleeve shirts.
7. Most of us still change into shorts when we get home from school.
8. The foggy season is here.
9. We have foggy day schedules for school. When a foggy day schedule is called we go to school at 10:00.
10. We wear warm clothes mainly in the mornings.
11. We just finished the harvest of pumpkins, walnuts, pomegranates, persimmons, and cotton.
12. We haven't even receive rain yet, maybe later this year.
13. We just finished national book week and the Great American Smoke Out.
14. The average temperature here is still about 75 degrees.
15. Most people plant winter rye grass because our bermuda grass is dormant. The rye grass stays pretty green all winter long.
16. We read books on cool evenings.
17. We eat popcorn and watch movies more at night.
18. Dew covers the cars, trees, plants, and grass every morning.
19. Some plants don't grow until spring.
20. Youth basketball is starting.

21. High School basketball is starting.
22. Soccer season is over.
23. Days get shorter.
24. We collect coats for kids that don't have any.

Thanks from Roosevelt School!

The challenge in this activity, of course, is not just to make lists and match similar items. It is to see and feel what November is like in a different part of the country. As Fred Newmann (1991) pointed out, it can be a formidable cognitive task to encounter someone else's experiences indirectly and attempt to understand them. This is happening at some level in Kathy's classroom: She reports that there was fog in Philadelphia in mid-December, and her students mentioned that it would be nice if they had foggy-day schedules like the children in California have.

In our view, Kathy's entry point to what Henry Giroux (1994, p. 42) calls "encounters with otherness" is just right. Children at age 9 can be helped rather easily to see that whereas they contend with frost, snow, and ice in early November, other children their age who live in a warmer climate do not. A discussion of differences in climate can lead to discussion of other differences—of language, gender, social class, and race, for instance. The latter set of differences can be much more difficult to discuss thoughtfully, without what Lisa Delpit (1995) called "name calling and labelling" (pp. 177–178), for, unlike climate, these differences have ideology (i.e., a system of beliefs about what people are like, what actions have value) and "isms" (e.g., sexism, racism) associated with them.

Failure of individuals and entire communities to be thoughtful in their encounters with otherness has dreadful social consequences, often for children. In his new book, *Amazing Grace: The Lives of Children and the Conscience of a Nation,* Jonathan Kozol (1995) reminded us that many people believe that poverty and the suffering that poor people endure can be blamed, for the most part, on their own "behaviors." With this assessment of blame, indifference to poverty becomes defensible, even when young children are involved. One of Kozol's many examples of indifference comes from an Arizona woman, who says about Mexican children, "I didn't breed them. I don't want to feed them" (p. 128).

## Linking Mail to Current Events

In Kathy Nell's class, part of developing empathy for students in unfamiliar places (crossing space and culture, in Newmann's [1991] terms) is linking everyday messages to breaking news. In "A Note from the Teacher" on the Web, Kathy and her class tell readers that they have heard from most of the United States, Canada, and Australia. This fall, the children in Kathy's class who have been corresponding with children in Canada were able to learn about Quebec's referendum on separation from the rest of Canada and to learn about it from the Canadian children's perspective.

It is so much easier for fourth graders (and adults, for that matter) to engage in critical analysis of a complex issue such as separatism when they have access to more than one perspective. It is difficult to question assertions provided by only one source (e.g., a CNN commentator's claiming that "If Quebec secedes, Canada will no longer be able to compete in world markets" or "Quebec's becoming a separate, French-speaking state will encourage ethnic minorities around the world to separate"), easier if one can compare sources (possibly television commentators from the United States and from both Toronto and Montreal). Given multiple sources, one can seek compelling evidence from each, noting likely bias in each.

## Using the Web to Learn About Historic Philadelphia

Kathy and her students live in an historic city—one that can boast of having the oldest bank, oldest hospital, and oldest continuously inhabited street in the United States. We knew that Philadelphia has been immensely important in the history of this country, of course, but we did not know about the bank, hospital, and street; those things we learned by clicking on links on the Forrest Elementary home page, just as Kathy's students can do in doing historical research about the city in which they live today.

This use of the Web is related to Newmann's (1991) description of empathy as the expansion of students' social experience across time, as an attempt to incorporate the experience of those who lived 2 centuries ago into our thinking. On the Web pages labeled "Philadelphia Historic District," one learns all of these things:

1. Before a bank of the United States was formed, each state had a different form of currency.
2. Philadelphia was the nation's capital when Alexander Hamilton suggested that such a national bank be built.
3. The bank cost about $110,000. to build.
4. Benjamin Franklin raised money to help found the oldest U.S. hospital.

5. Originally, the top floor of the east wing was for men, the ground floor for women, the basement for the mentally ill.
6. Upstairs, in the operating amphitheater, the first appendicitis and gall bladder surgery in the U.S. was performed.
7. In historic Philadelphia, the dwellings in center city were owned by prosperous merchants. Middle-class families lived to the north by the Delaware River.

These seven facts alone do not tell us much about life in Philadelphia 2 centuries ago. After all, as Kathyrn and Luther Spoehr (1994) reminded us, learning to think historically—Kathy Nell's goal for her students—does not mean knowing more facts than anyone else: "Focusing exclusively on facts is what makes history study so deadly dull for so many students in so many schools; students get the idea that history is just one damn thing after another, and that their job is to memorize as many facts as possible, preferably in chronological order" (p. 71).

The reason that the facts are useful is that they help fill in a picture of what events were associated with each other at a particular point in time—for example, development of a nation and formation of a national bank to standardize currency; particular views about mental illness and layout of the first hospital that segregated mental patients from other patients; social class, one's standing in the community, and place of residence in the historic city. Because of some of the features we highlighted earlier about the Web (i.e., one can move from a document to background information, some information is pictorial so we can see pictures of the first bank or oldest street, the learner controls browsing through information), it is an ideal tool for seeking associations, for looking for meaningful connections among bits of information.

# GETTING AROUND ORGANIZATIONAL OBSTACLES TO BECOME WEB-ACTIVE

Fred Newmann (1991) thinks that quite a few teachers want to do the sorts of things that Kathy Nell is doing to develop empathy in her students. They want to use the Web, to nudge their students away from being passive recipients of volumes of textbook information. They want to devise means by which their students and students in a different place can correspond about everyday events and about big news stories such as the Quebec referendum. They want to have fun at the computer along with in-depth, thoughtful discussions about "encounters with otherness."

But there are obstacles: Large classes and lean resources make browsing, composing and peer-editing at the computer difficult; guidelines for content coverage induce guilt in teachers if they spend many days on a single topic or activity, so there are many teachers who choose not to engage in Web work; and 50-minute periods break up thoughtful discussions about difference (and just about anything else).

And those are just the obstacles within the school district. There are problems with the Web as well, as Gerry Stahl, Tamara Sumner, and Robert Owen (1995) reminded us. "Teachers wandering around the Internet looking for ideas to use in their classrooms" (Stahl et al., p. 237) confront problems even when they are knowledgeable about the Internet. Two are: (a) No system announces the locations of curriculum ideas scattered across the network; and (b) different interfaces, tools, and indexing schemes are used within each site where ideas are located. Busy teachers need browsing mechanisms that help them select curricula of interest efficiently. The good news is that some mechanisms are in development phase right now (see Gillingham, 1996, for an example). The bad news is that some standardization (e.g., of resource indexing) will be required to make the mechanisms workable.

As to within-district obstacles, Kathy has been able to get around them, in part, because of the way in which she conceives of her work: She is an advocate for substantial autonomy among teachers. Rather than waiting for district allocation of resources, she has dragged her own computer and modem to school. She has sought teachers from whom she can learn and with whom she can collaborate on the Web. She works outside traditional blocks of instructional time, allowing children to work at the two computers before school and at lunch and during recess time.

And, perhaps most significantly, she is so clear about the knowledge, skills, and dispositions that she wants the children to develop in social studies (and literature) that she can follow the exchanges on the Web, the interests of the children ("Whatever develops from the students' interest is usually where I go") in devising specific activities for any given week. This is bold, confident, pedagogy-savvy, content-rich teaching that, even among very experienced teachers, is rare.

Having told stories about six innovative teachers and six sets of classroom events, we turn, in chapter 8, to a discussion of patterns. We describe continuity across the six classrooms.

# III

Patterns

# 8

# Continuity Across Classrooms

In our six cases, we were surprised to see considerable continuity across contexts, despite obvious differences such as size of community, age of students, experience of teacher, and efficiency of electronic equipment. In this final chapter, we note four general patterns that emerged.

## BOTH STUDENTS AND TEACHERS TELL STORIES

One clear pattern is the use of stories. In thinking about stories, we are reminded of Herbert Kohl's (1995) anecdote about his visit to a high school classroom in which violence in the school was being discussed in a loud and animated manner. Every student, it seems, had something to say. The teacher, in an effort to focus the discussion, asked the students to tell their stories briefly, to get to the point. After this admonition, the students fell silent. The stories they had to tell were the point for them. They wanted to tell personal details, not to summarize. As Kohl noted, it would have been wise for the teacher to allow the discussion to continue the next day, to let it take up the curriculum space that the importance of the topic and the interest of the students demanded.

Herbert Kohl (1995) went on to say that each school year can be considered a story too, and the telling of the story can be a valuable form of reflection for teachers. Many educational researchers would agree. Kathy Carter (1993), for instance, linked teachers' stories to reflection in action, to an understanding of one's practice. Both sorts of stories appear in our cases—students' stories about everyday events and teachers' stories about classroom events.

Most of the students' stories would be characterized by Shirley Brice Heath (1983) as "true stories" (p. 158), based on real events and rich in image-evoking detail. In Ruth Coleman's class, Jadine tells about being accused by her grandmother of stealing $2, and Edward tells about a neighborhood fire that he and his friend noticed and called in to the fire department. In Chris Meier's class, Gerald tells about playing lap game and catching geese; David tells about ptarmigan hunting with his father; and Grace tells about climbing the rock people and seeing the entire village, the pond, and the ocean from the top. In Hugh Dyment's class, Sebastian and Anthony tell their former teachers all about "blowing" the basketball tournament game against Toksook. And, in Kathy Nell's class, Megan tells a moving story about the death of Max, her dog. Memory, detail, fact, and feeling combine, it seems, to produce powerful student stories.

Most of the teachers' stories are also "true stories," well-remembered events interpreted at close range. From the stream of experience of entire school days and weeks, some classroom events are more salient than others, and it is about those that teachers tell stories. Some of the stories are technical (e.g., Kathy Plamondon's telling how KIDCAFE participants must prepare a Response to Four Questions before they can participate in the List), whereas others touch not only on classroom decision-making, but also on teachers' life histories (e.g., Daniel Wilcox's commenting on the unpredictability and uncertainty of students' responses to books that he teaches from one year to the next, but adding that "students have learned best when I introduced a work of literature that I loved"). In much of what Daniel and Hugh shared with each other, we see teaching method and curriculum decisions mixed in with personal goals and philosophies.

We relied on Jerome Bruner's (1990) *Acts of Meaning* in Chapter 3 (and at many other points in this book) in an effort to understand why narrative is so often the vehicle that both students and teachers choose in their attempts to communicate with each other. There is something about the way that narrative organizes experience that seems to appeal to most of us.

Perhaps it is what Bruner calls its "inherent sequentiality" (p. 43), which does make stories easy to understand and remember. Story plot, whether factual (as in "true stories" and in accounts provided by historians) or fictional (as in imaginative tales woven by novelists) is always a sequence of events: One thing happens, and then something else happens. In telling about the action, narrators have the opportunity to tell something about intention, about what characters in the story (often they) believe and want.

Narratives are really quite predictable—if not in content, at least in form. They usually begin with a specification of the time, and sometimes the place, in which the story took place:

> . . . There was state troopers in town yesterday. They were looking for people because they broke the law. . . . (Elizabeth A. in Chris Meier's class)

Characters are introduced early:

> . . . Well first of all, Tununak is doing great. Juniors and Seniors and some young adults are getting ready for confirmation. We take classes every Wednesday evening for two hours. Some young adults who are joining us are taking classes with us because they weren't confirmed last year or the past years. During our first class with Dick Lincoln, Sophie Oscar, and Father Peter, we were too quiet. I guess we were too shy to ask questions because it was our first time, and we just sat there and listened to Father Peter's lecture. . . . (Bobbiann in Hugh Dyment's class)

And, as we have said, things happen, one after the other:

> . . . Most of the students crowded up and sat on the floor, only several still in their desks, a good sign. I raised Elie's question: Why do bad things, terrible things, evil things happen to people? Then I gave them several recent examples besides the faroff one of Nazis killing babies. I mentioned the LA earthquake, the little girl killed by gang violence, and a boy that died of cancer. I reminded them of the GB rules: teacher doesn't give his answers, all answers receive credit, though teacher may press for supporting evidence. Surprise! Two hands shot up; deep thoughts were shared about why bad things happened to people. Soon it snowballed and I had a line of hands waiting to share their thoughts on the topic. . . . (Daniel Wilcox)

But the real appeal of stories, the reason why we seem to prefer them to other forms of discourse, may be that they belong to us. When we tell a story, *we* decide how to introduce characters, which events to divulge, and what to make of our character and of the role we play in events. Children, who are just beginning their narrative careers, already seem to understand this. Jadine, in Ruth Coleman's class, surely understands:

> . . . My grandmother accuses me of everything. I had my baby sister on my shoulder and my grandmother told my cousin to take my sister away from me. DO you have any sisters or brothers? One day my grandmother said I stole two dollars. . . .

David, in Chris Meier's class, also seems to understand:

... My Dad and I went to look for some ptarmigan. I saw a ptarmigan. But we did not shoot the ptarmigan because it was going fast.

And, Jennifer, in Kathy Plamondon's class, seems to understand too:

... I love going over to my Bestfriends's house her name is Bess. I am five foot six, golden brown hair and have very unusual colored eyes. Bess said they look as if there red crosses with a greenish brown back ground. ...

## INTERNET ACTIVITY IS VERY SOCIAL

A second pattern that emerges in our cases is the highly social nature of Internet communication. The students and teachers who sit at computers pecking out stories of events in their lives are quite obviously intent on telling the stories to others in the global village, not on storing them in the recesses of the machine. Sherry Turkle, professor of the Sociology of Science at MIT, described her own intentions in front of the computer in a recent *Wired* profile by Pamela McCorduck (1996):

Ten years ago, people who were very involved with computers were geeks—it was pejorative. Now we're coming into a phase of the hacker as hunk. It has to do with the cultural associations computers have: now it's not surprising that people like me, who are interested in people, in politics, in the world at large, are also into computers. (p. 162)

Fred Erickson (1981) told us some time ago that humans do not talk simply for the sake of talking. (He was surely referring to face-to-face or telephone conversation in 1981, but we think that the point holds for Internet communication as well.) Humans talk to accomplish social purposes (e.g., to impart or seek information, to amuse or be amused, to persuade or be persuaded). Anne Lamott (1994) said much the same thing more recently: "You begin to string words together like beads to tell a story. You are desperate to communicate, to edify or entertain, to preserve moments of grace or joy or transcendence, to make real or imagined events come alive." (p. 7.)

From these perspectives, the Internet conversations are like other forms of communication in their socialness.

One reason why we have characterized Internet communication as "conversations written down" (Heath, 1983, p. 213) throughout this book is that in the exchange of ideas from classroom to classroom, turns are taken, as in most conversation: A speaks and B listens, and then B speaks and A listens. A and B often repeat each other's words and ideas. Sometimes either A or B will flash what in face-to-face conversation would be a quizzical glance at the other. All of this is very social, very interactive.

We have many examples of this sort of thing. We provide but one here, which begins as A (Grace in Chris Meier's class) speaks, and B (Doris in Ruth Coleman's class) listens:

> . . . We have rock people. I speak Yupik. IF you want to climb up to the rock people you will have to wear you rubber boots. Yesterday I went up to the rock people. . . .

Then, B (Doris) speaks, and A (Grace) listens. Doris flashes an electronic quizzical glance along the lines of "Huh? What are these rock people?" as part of her message:

> I want to know what you mean when you say "rock people". What are they? We guessed that they are rocks that look like people. Can you climb on them? . . .

Then, it is back to A (Grace) speaking, B (Doris) listening:

> The rock people are just a pile of rocks, flat rocks. If you go up you will see the whole village and the pond and ocean. And you will be scared. At the rock people it is cool. If you go down to the village after you were cold, and if you go down it will be hot.

In addition to turn taking, which gives Internet communication a conversational feel, there is also considerable self-disclosure. In reading some of the messages in the various classrooms, one can almost hear a conversational voice drop to a whisper, while something rather—uh, private—is revealed. The high school students in Hugh Dyment's class are particularly self-disclosing (about college choice anxiety, losing a big game, goofing off in school, and so forth). Recalling that the Internet communication is between the high school students and admired non-Eskimo adults who no longer live in the village, Hugh suggests that the students are afforded a rare opportunity to step outside their reserved and polite culture, to talk quite openly about adolescent anxieties and insecurities.

There are, obviously, enormous individual and cultural differences in conversational style but, in general, most of us divulge quite a bit to most of our Internet correspondents, who are relative strangers, after all. We now know, for instance, something about Chris Meier's plans for more graduate work; we know a really harrowing story about one of Hugh's students who had a crisis during the senior career field trip this fall; we know that Kathy Plamondon had a fire in her house while doing some art work unrelated to her teaching; and we know that Daniel Wilcox gets chided, nightly, to quit his e-mail and get some sleep. All of the teachers know something about our difficulties in juggling writing with day-to-day academic administration and they know that when we can steal away for good jazz on a weekend, we do so.

There is no denying that the medium promotes social behavior. Daniel's explanation for this is that the Internet is much like traveling (we like this analogy; it reminds us of Fred Newmann's point about expanding students' social experience across time, space, and culture, which one does in both travel and in Internet communication). Daniel continues:

> When I hitch-hiked across Europe in the early 70's I often had deep conversations with relative strangers who I had only known for minutes. I still remember discussing the nature of reality and whether God exists with a bunch of travelers in a hostel somewhere in Germany late into the night. ... I think it's being out of the rut and the knowing that if you goof [disclose too much? say something stupid? offend unintentionally?] it's not like the person is your next door neighbor who is going to flame you every day when you come outside. . . .

We agree with Daniel's analysis, especially the part about the built-in protection of distance.

Batya Friedman (1991) was mentioned earlier in this book. She argued that e-mail and bulletin boards invite social activity because they encourage participants to share ideas and discuss issues of common interest—exactly what we have observed. And, Paul Saffo, a California computer industry consultant, described the Web as "television colliding with the telephone party line . . . community with a vengeance" (Markoff, 1995, p. 5C). There is some of that in our cases too—for instance, Kathy Nell's students' poetry on the Web accompanied by photos of the poets and envelope icons as prompts to readers to write back with personal responses. Anyone on the Web (the party line) can read the poems and view the pictures (the television), and then decide to write back.

Social consequences of long-term communication on the Internet are potentially enormous: Cultural stereotypes yield to more accurate information (e.g., children in Ruth Coleman's classroom in Joliet learn that some Eskimos live on soggy tundra rather than in igloos near glacial fjords). Extended "encounters with otherness" occur (e.g., in Kathy Nell's classroom, children learn that their California correspondents are more worried about fog than about snow and ice in November, and that there may not be homeless people sleeping on grates in Dinuba like there are in downtown Philadelphia).

## THE TECHNOLOGY
## IS MORE OR LESS INVISIBLE

This is a book about teachers, students, and communication. It is *not* about bits of information, bandwidth, or baud rate. If the technology in the classrooms that we have observed is not particularly noticeable, that is a good thing, for it means that users are, as Christina Haas (1996) put it, not so much looking *at* the computer as looking *through* it to the task at hand. It means that the technology is allowing students and teachers to focus on making rhetorical choices (e.g., how informal to be in a first e-mail message or how much to elaborate in a subsequent one, how much more to revise a message for publication on the Web) rather than worrying about the innards of various pieces of equipment. It means that ideas are moving across time, space, and culture without much of a hitch.

The point at which the technology becomes visible to most of us—certainly to Ruth, Hugh, and Daniel, who have written about this recently—is when it ceases to function normally, when there is a fracture in the long chain of links from person A to person B. There are many links: the local telephone company that provides a dialtone and switching to person A; the Internet service provider that provides lines from A's telephone company (and modems, servers, routers, bridges, and gateways, all of which contain software that requires maintenance and can malfunction); regional lines from the provider to the Internet line; and intermediate carriers that cross regions along an often convoluted path to regional lines for B; the Internet service provider for B; and last, the local telephone company for B.

Machines must not only function independently; they must engage in what computer insiders call "handshaking." Handshaking sounds almost human when described by Nicholas Negroponte (1995): It is two machines establishing communication, deciding on variables to be used in conversations. He adds, "Just listen to your fax or data modem next time you use it. All that staticky-sounding noise and the beeps are literally the handshaking process. These mating calls are negotiations to find the highest terrain from which they can trade bits . . . " (p. 207)

Daniel Wilcox is in the same situation as many of us, having escalated his use of the Internet from infrequent to very frequent: He is distressed when something goes wrong with some part of the system, frustrated about, among other things, not being able to send or receive messages. This frustration is apparent in just some of the messages he sent in late October and early November:

> Hugh, this is a comedy of errors, but I am not laughing. This morning, for some reason my printer is not working. And I tried to install MS5—I dumped 6 last night because it froze again—but it won't install. It says something about a problem but that my software was saved.? I don't understand it; for I removed my disinfectant and extensions as instructed. Furthermore, my other computer which I was trying to network with, now won't display any icon when I load a disk. I am trying to send you some of your students' mail and the several of the narratives and essays. Let me know if they open. . . . (October 29)

> My printer is finally working again; unknown problem. However, now PPP is not working again. I don't know if it is the server or that I messed up the program trying to get Eudora to work last night. . . . (October 30)

> Config PPP opened, but the PPP won't open, says I don't have a translator. I presume the point is that I am still sending you files that you can't read, yes? Sorry. (later in the day, October 30)

> Please send me a binHex file to practice as you offered. That name makes me think of my American literature class; for we recently studied the Salem Witchcraft Trials. BixHex is listed at the top of this paper. How would I receive BinHex on eWorld or AOL? (October 31)

> Seriously, there is a problem. I can't find your attachments from your last two letters. Plus, I have been getting this box on my screen: Your attachments folder cannot be found. If you don't set a new one in the settings dialog, E. will use A.F. in your Eudora folder. I am reading page 39 of the manual and think I am going to figure it out. I guess I have to create a folder. It would be nice if we had someone who knew Eudora here in Santa Maria. Unfortunately, our librarian (who just learned it this last week) can't help me because she is moving to Salinas. And our server doesn't know much about Macs. So I am on my own except for the manual and you. . . . (November 1)

. . . Now that the district has spent 3 years planning to start a network, it has invested thousands of dollars in new LC computers for Santa Maria High, it has given us a little training, etc., etc., some teachers at the other high school are blocking the district from buying the final software necessary to set up the overdue network, because they think the money can be best spent elsewhere . . . But never fear, I the resourceful teacher have two modems now, one at school and one at home and I have a Syquest to jaunt between computers—so who needs a network, I have my own. I am happy, right? Wrong. Two thirds of the time I can't get on Eudora or Netscape because the County server is down . . . (November 15)

Nearly everything that Daniel mentions has happened to us—and no doubt to each of the teachers mentioned in this book. We have been every bit as frustrated as he has. We have noticed, in discussing these matters with academic colleagues, that a reasoned set of reactions to this state of affairs is out of the question. What actually occurs, in approximately the following order, is: (a) lighthearted joking about the problem (this step is of short duration); (b) vile verbal attacks on unspecified components of what, after all, remains a mostly mysterious system; (c) frenzied attempts at problem solving, which include reading nearly incomprehensible documentation and then rereading it and talking to anyone who might know anything about computers and the Internet—in Daniel's case, the librarian (until she moved to Salinas); (d) more of (b), but at a higher volume, and with considerably more feeling; and, finally, (e) subjecting small pieces of the system to odd rituals (e.g., shaking a floppy disk; turning the computer on before the printer and before pouring coffee rather than after; whispering incantations while loading up communications software). The oddest thing of all, of course, is that (a) to (d) almost never work, but (e) sometimes does. Our department secretary absolutely swears by the disk-shaking ritual.

## TEACHERS MAKE AN ENORMOUS DIFFERENCE

The six teachers in our cases are distinct individuals of course, but they have a handful of important characteristics in common: They are not very didactic or teacher-centered in their instruction, they link student interest to subject-matter learning, they view technology as a means rather than an end, and they believe that all of their students can succeed.

Perhaps most important of all, they each, in one way or another, seek alternatives to their current practice. They are intent on discovering new ways of helping students learn, welcoming rather than fearing newness and variety in their school lives. All teachers have what David Tyack and Larry Cuban (1995) called "an investment in the familiar institutional practices of the school" (p. 9)—the daily routines that we learn as students and take for granted when we move to the other side of the teacher's desk. However, some teachers (these six among them) are prepared to make some fundamental changes in the way they operate with students because they see a need to do so. They make changes from the inside out, often well in advance of significant support from their districts.

In part, it is an expanded repertoire of materials and methods that they seek: Ruth Coleman's wanting to relinquish some "red pencil" control, looking for ways to implement peer editing; both Chris Meier's and Hugh Dyment's seeking new ways for their L2 learners to practice speaking and writing in English; Kathy Plamondon's looking for ways to encourage open, but respectful, conversation in her classroom; and Daniel Wilcox's trying to figure out how to link Internet activity to other assignments.

In part, it is much more than materials and methods. It is wanting to think and talk with others about the "big issues" (why they wanted to teach in the first place, why they still do despite tremendous challenges). This is conversation about teacher conceptions, not teacher actions. In this context, Hugh's and Daniel's exchanges are particularly revealing. They began talking about *Night,* but moved quickly to talking about personal and professional goals as well:

I forgot to mention in my last rant that I wouldn't give up teaching in a village right now for anything. I need variety and excitement as I bore easily. . . . (Hugh)

. . . The big push here is in school to job, career paths, and I'm not against students finding a career early and improving their lot in life. I certainly wouldn't want them to follow in my footsteps, careening around the world for 10 years after high school. But having students select paths before they have even asked the great questions seems to be one of the weaknesses of current educational mania; it just sucks 9th graders into the lie that money and job is all. (Daniel)

. . . This shows where personal experience weighs more in how a teacher teaches than his educational readings. I always wanted long and detailed comments on my papers and so think I need to give them to my students. . . . (Daniel)

. . . Public school districts are top heavy with management, are encumbered with red tape and are regulated to death. . . . (Hugh)

The teachers in our cases even reflect on and discuss flawed or failed pedagogy. Ruth Coleman worries about the delay in sending and receiving messages because she had, until recently, no Internet connection in her classroom. Chris Meier regrets having tampered with his students' messages to Illinois. Kathy Plamondon feels bad that it took so long to "hook" Paula on oral and written communication activities. Daniel Wilcox ponders why his interpretive movie project elicited only a 65% submission rate in one class this year.

And, always, they move in search of the global village of words and images, of ideas, from beyond their immediate experience. Jim Cummins and Dennis Sayers (1995) wrote about tribal instincts and about fear of difference. The alternatives to fear of difference, they say (and we agree), are communicating and learning.

We do not have the sense about any of the teachers in our cases that they are working in truly extraordinary settings (i.e., unusually well-equipped buildings housing just the right number of eager students and collaborative colleagues). Rather, what emerges from each case is a picture of a talented teacher doing really good work in a rather ordinary setting. Some resources exist, some are only hoped for; some students are highly engaged, others not so much; and there is some collaboration, but not as much as the teachers might want. They have found peers who want to experiment with and within this new medium, but they have usually found them outside the walls of their own buildings.

Herbert Kohl (1986) began his introduction to the 1986 edition of *On Teaching* by writing that the fundamentals of good teaching do not change all that much. Good teaching has always been—as Richard Elmore, Penelope Peterson, and Sarah McCarthey (1996) reminded us recently—very difficult and demanding work. What changes, Kohl argued, is that there are times when teachers find their work appreciated and other times when the same work is devalued. These times do not strike us as particularly appreciative ones. We think that one important reason for teachers to seek out other teachers with whom they can talk—to seek global community—is that they need to remind each other how caring, knowledgeable, and ingenious they really are.

# References

Anderson, L. M., Brubaker, N. L., Alleman-Brooks, J., & Duffy, G. G. (1985). A qualitative study of seatwork in first-grade classrooms. *Elementary School Journal, 86,* 123–140.

Applebee, A. N. (1991). Informal reasoning and writing instruction. In J. F. Voss, D. N. Perkins, & J. W. Segal (Eds.), *Informal reasoning and education* (pp. 401–414). Hillsdale, NJ: Lawrence Erlbaum Associates.

Ashton-Warner, S. (1986). *Teacher.* New York: Simon & Shuster.

Au, K. H., Mason, J. M., & Scheu, J. A. (1995). *Literacy instruction for today.* New York: HarperCollins.

Ayers, W. (1993). *To teach: The journey of a teacher.* New York: Teachers College Press.

Baron, J. (1991). Beliefs about thinking. In J. F. Voss, D. N. Perkins, & J. W. Segal (Eds.), *Informal reasoning and education* (pp. 169–186). Hillsdale, NJ: Lawrence Erlbaum Associates.

Becker, H. J. (1995, December). *Schools of the national school network testbed: Current Internet use.* Paper presented at the fourth international conference on Telecommunications in Education, Fort Lauderdale, FL.

Borko, H., Eisenhart, M., Brown, C. A., Underhill, R. G., Jones, D., & Agard, P. C. (1992). Learning to teach hard mathematics: Do novice teachers and their instructors give up too easily? *Journal for Research in Mathematics Education, 23,* 194–222.

Broudy, H. S. (1990). Case studies—Why and how. *Teachers College Record, 91,* 449–459.

Bruce, B. C., & Rubin, A. (1993). *Electronic quills: A situated evaluation of using computers for writing in classroom.* Hillsdale, NJ: Lawrence Erlbaum Associates.

Bruner, J. (1990). *Acts of meaning.* Cambridge, MA: Harvard University Press.

**139**

Carter, K. (1993). The place of story in the study of teaching and teacher education. *Educational Researcher, 22,* 5–12, 18.

Carver, R. (1992). *Will you please be quiet, please?* New York: Vintage.

Caufield, C. (1990, May 14). *The ancient forest.* New Yorker, 46–50, 52, 56, 58, 60–62, 64–72, 74–84.

Cazden, C. B. (1988). *Classroom discourse: The language of teaching and learning.* Portsmouth, NH: Heinemann.

Chambliss, M. J. (1994). Why do readers fail to change their beliefs after reading persuasive text? In R. Garner & P. A. Alexander (Eds.), *Beliefs about text and about instruction with text* (pp. 75–89). Hillsdale, NJ: Lawrence Erlbaum Associates.

Cohen, D. K. (1988). Educational technology and school organization. In R. Nickerson & P. P. Zodhiates (Eds.), *Technology in education: Looking toward 2020* (pp. 231–264). Hillsdale, NJ: Lawrence Erlbaum Associates.

Cohen, M., & Riel, M. (1989). The effect of distant audiences on students' writing. *American Educational Research Journal, 26,* 143–159.

Connelly, F. M., & Clandinin, D. J. (1990). Stories of experience and narrative inquiry. *Educational Researcher, 19,* 2–14.

Crismore, A. (1989). Rhetorical form, selection and use of textbooks. In S. de Castell, A. Luke, & C. Luke (Eds.), *Language, authority and criticism: Readings on the school textbook* (pp. 133–152). London: Falmer.

Cuban, L. (1992). What happens to reforms that last? The case of the junior high school. *American Educational Research Journal, 29,* 227–251.

Cummins, J., & Sayers, D. (1995). *Brave new schools: Challenging cultural illiteracy through global learning networks.* New York: St. Martin's Press.

Delpit, L. (1995). *Other people's children: Cultural conflict in the classroom.* New York: New Press.

Dewey, J. (1900). *The school and society.* Chicago: University of Chicago Press.

Editorial. (1995, September). *New York Times,* p. 12A.

Edwards, A. D., & Westgate, D. P. G. (1994). *Investigating classroom talk* (2nd ed.). London: Falmer.

Ellsworth, J. (1994). *Education on the Internet.* Indianapolis, IN: Sams Publishing.

Elmer-Dewitt, P. (1995, July 3). On a screeen near you: Cyberporn. *Time,* 38–45.

Elmore, R. F., Peterson, P. L., & McCarthey, S. J. (1996). *Restructuring in the classroom: Teaching, learning, and school organization.* San Francisco, CA: Jossey-Bass.

Erickson, F. (1981). Timing and context in everyday discourse: Implications for the study of referential and social meaning. In W. P. Dickson (Ed.), *Children's oral communication skills* (pp. 241–269). New York: Academic.

Fienup-Riordan, A. (1990). *Eskimo essays: Yup'ik lives and how we see them.* New Brunswick, NJ: Rutgers University Press.

Fine, M. (1993). "You can't just say that the only ones who can speak are those who agree with your position": Political discourse in the classroom. *Harvard Educational Review, 63,* 412–433.

Flavell, J. H., Miller, P. H., & Miller, S. A. (1993). *Cognitive development* (3rd ed.). Englewood Cliffs, NJ: Prentice-Hall.

Florio-Ruane, S. (1987). Sociolinguistics for educational researchers. *American Educational Research Journal, 24,* 185–197.

Flynn, L. (1995, September 11). Apple holds school market, despite decline. *The New York Times,* p. 5C.

Friedman, B. (1991). Social and moral development through computer use: A constructivist approach. *Journal of Research on Computing in Education, 23,* 560–567.

Gardner, H. (1991). *The unschooled mind.* New York: Basic Books.

Garner, R. (1987). *Metacognition and reading comprehension.* Norwood, NJ: Ablex.

Garner, R. (1990). When children and adults do not use learning strategies: Toward a theory of settings. *Review of Educational Research, 60,* 517–529.

Garner, R., & Alexander, P. A. (1994). Preface. In R. Garner & P. A. Alexander (Eds.), *Beliefs about text and instruction with text* (pp. xvii–xxii). Hillsdale, NJ: Lawrence Erlbaum Associates.

Garner, R., & Hansis, R. (1994). Literacy practices outside of school: Adults' beliefs and their responses to "street texts." In R. Garner & P. A. Alexander (Eds.), *Beliefs about text and instruction with text* (pp. 57–73). Hillsdale, NJ: Lawrence Erlbaum Associates.

Gillingham, M. G. (1996, April). *Organizing the World Wide Web for teachers: Hypertextual database strategies.* Paper presented at the annual meeting of the American Educational Research Association, New York.

Gillingham, M. G., Young, M. F., & Kulikowich, J. M. (1994). Do teachers consider nonlinear text to be text? In R. Garner & P. A. Alexander (Eds.), *Beliefs about text and instruction with text* (pp. 201–219). Hillsdale, NJ: Lawrence Erlbaum Associates.

Giroux, H. A. (1994). Living dangerously: Identity politics and the new cultural racism. In H. A. Giroux & P. McLaren (Eds.), *Between borders: Pedagogy and the politics of cultural studies* (pp. 29–55). New York: Routledge.

Goodman, S. (1994). Talking back: The portrait of a student documentary on school inequity. In F. Pignatelli & S. W. Pflaum (Eds.), *Experiencing diversity: Toward educational equity* (pp. 47–69). Thousand Oaks, CA: Corwin.

Greene, M. (1993). The passions of pluralism: Multiculturalism and the expanding community. In T. Perry & J. W. Fraser (Eds.), *Freedom's plow: Teaching in the multicultural classroom* (pp. 185–196). New York: Routledge.

Grumet, M. R. (1987). The politics of personal knowledge. *Curriculum Inquiry, 17,* 319–329.

Gudmundsdottir, S. (1995). The narrative nature of pedagogical content knowledge. In H. McEwan & K. Egan (Eds.), *Narrative in teaching, learning, and research* (pp. 24–38). New York: Teachers College Press.

Haas, C. (1996). *Writing technology: Studies on the materiality of literacy.* Mahwah, NJ: Lawrence Erlbaum Associates.

Heath, S. B. (1983). *Ways with words: Language, life, and work in communities and classrooms.* Cambridge, England: Cambridge University Press.

Heaviside, S., Farris, E., Malitz, G., & Carpenter, J. (1995). *Advanced telecommunications in U.S. public schools, K–12* (Publication No. NCES 95–731). Washington, DC: U.S. Government Printing Office.

Henze, R. C., & Vanett, L. (1993). To walk in two worlds—Or more? Challenging a common metaphor of Native education. *Anthropology and Education Quarterly, 24,* 116–134.

Jackson, P. W. (1990). *Life in classrooms.* New York: Teachers College Press.

Jacob, E. (1995). Reflective practice and anthropology in culturally diverse classrooms. *Elementary School Journal, 95,* 451–463.

Kagan, D. M. (1993). Contexts for the use of classroom cases. *American Educational Research Journal, 30,* 703–723.

Kidder, T. (1989). *Among schoolchildren.* Boston, MA: Houghton Mifflin.

Kohl, H. (1986). *On teaching.* New York: Schocken Books.

Kohl, H. (1995). *Should we burn Babar? Essays on children's literature and the power of stories.* New York: New Press.

Kozol, J. (1991). *Savage inequalities: Children in America's schools.* New York: Crown.

Kozol, J. (1995). *Amazing grace: The lives of children and the conscience of a nation.* New York: Crown.

Ladson-Billings, G. (1994). *The dreamkeepers: Successful teachers of African American children.* San Francisco, CA: Jossey-Bass.

Lagemann, E. C. (1991). Talk about teaching. *Teachers College Record, 93,* 1–5.

Lamott, A. (1994). *Bird by bird: Some instructions on writing and life.* New York: Pantheon.

Lebowitz, F. (1981). *Social studies.* New York: Random House.

Levine, L. (1993). "Who says?" Learning to value diversity in school. In F. Pignatelli & S. W. Pflaum (Eds.), *Celebrating diverse voices: Progressive education and equity* (pp. 87–111). Newbury Park, CA: Corwin.

LeVine, R. (1982). Culture, context, and the concept of development. In W. A. Collins (Ed.), *The concept of development: The Minnesota symposia on child psychology* (Vol. 15, pp. 162–166). Hillsdale, NJ: Lawrence Erlbaum Associates.

Lieberman, A. (1992). The meaning of scholarly activity and the building of community. *Educational Researcher, 21,* 5–12.

Lohr, S. (1995, September 21). Protecting youngsters from Internet dangers. *The New York Times,* pp. 1–2B.

Luke, A. (1995). Text and discourse in education: An introduction to critical discourse analysis. In M. W. Apple (Ed.), *Review of Research in Education* (Vol. 21, pp. 3–48). Washington, DC: American Educational Research Association.

Luke, C., de Castell, S., & Luke, A. (1983). Beyond criticism: The authority of the school text. *Curriculum Inquiry, 13,* 111–127.

Markoff, J. (1995, November 20). If medium is the message, the message is the Web. *The New York Times,* pp. 1A, 5C.

McCorduck, P. (1996, April). Sex, lies, and avatars. *Wired,* 106–111, 158, 160–162, 164–165.

McLuhan, M. (1964). *Understanding media: The extensions of man.* New York: McGraw-Hill.

Mehan, H. (1995). Resisting the politics of despair. *Anthropology and Education Quarterly, 26,* 239–250.

Meier, D. (1995). *The power of their ideas: Lessons for America from a small school in Harlem.* Boston, MA: Beacon Press.

Merseth, K. K. (1992). Cases for decision making in teacher education. In J. H. Shulman (Ed.), *Case methods in teacher education* (pp. 50–63). New York: Teachers College Press.

Miller, P. H. (1983). *Theories of developmental psychology.* San Francisco, CA: W. H. Freeman.

Moore, L. (1990). *Like life.* New York: Alfred A. Knopf.

Mosle, S. (1995a, May 28). A city school experiment that actually works. *The New York Times Magazine,* pp. 26–31, 49–51.

Mosle, S. (1995b, September 18). Writing down secrets. *New Yorker,* 52–55, 58–61.

Negroponte, N. (1995). *Being digital.* New York: Alfred A. Knopf.

Newmann, F. M. (1991). Higher order thinking in the teaching of social studies: Connections between theory and practice. In J. F. Voss, D. N. Perkins, & J. W. Segal (Eds.), *Informal reasoning and education* (pp. 381–400). Hillsdale, NJ: Lawrence Erlbaum Associates.

Nystrand, M. (1989). A social-interactive model of writing. *Written Communication, 6,* 66–85.

Office of Technology Assessment. (1995). *Teachers and technology: Making the connection* (Publication No. OTA–EHR–616). Washington, DC: U.S. Government Printing Office.

Olson, J. (1988). *Schoolworlds/Microworlds: Computers and the culture of the classroom.* Oxford: Pergamon.

Papert, S. (1980). *Mindstorms: Children, computers, and powerful ideas.* New York: Basic Books.

Peck, W. C., Flower, L., & Higgins, L. (1995). Community literacy. *College Composition and Communication, 46,* 199–222.

Peterson, P. L. (1994). Research studies as texts: Sites for exploring the beliefs and learning of researchers and teachers. In R. Garner & P. A. Alexander (Eds.), *Beliefs about text and instruction with text* (pp. 93–120). Hillsdale, NJ: Lawrence Erlbaum Associates.

Postman, N. (1979). *Teaching as a conserving activity.* New York: Delacorte.

Postman, N. (1993). *Technopoly: The surrender of culture to technology.* New York: Vintage.

Renninger, K. A. (1992). Individual interest and development: Implications for theory and practice. In K. A. Renninger, S. Hidi, & A. Krapp (Eds.), *The role of interest in learning and development* (pp. 361–395). Hillsdale, NJ: Lawrence Erlbaum Associates.

Rheingold, H. (1994). *The virtual community: Homesteading on the electronic frontier.* New York: Harper Perennial.

Richardson, V. (1990). Significant and worthwhile change in teaching practice. *Educational Researcher, 19,* 10–18.

Riel, M. (1990). Cooperative learning across classrooms in electronic Learning Circles. *Instructional Science, 19,* 445–466.

Riel, M. (1994). Educational change in a technology-rich environment. *Journal of Research on Computing in Education, 26,* 452–474.

Romero, O. (1994). Bilingual education: A double-edged sword in the struggle for equity. In F. Pignatelli & S. W. Pflaum (Eds.), *Experiencing diversity: Toward educational equity* (pp. 82–95). Thousand Oaks, CA: Corwin.

Rubin, A. (1980). A theoretical taxonomy of the differences between oral and written language. In R. J. Spiro, B. C. Bruce, & W. F. Brewer (Eds.), *Theoretical issues in reading comprehension* (pp. 411–438). Hillsdale, NJ: Lawrence Erlbaum Associates.

Schank, R. C., & Cleary, C. (1994). *Engines for education.* Evanston, IL: Northwestern University, Institute for the Learning Sciences.

Schank, R. C., & Osgood, R. E. (1993). *The communications story* (Tech. Rep. No. 37). Evanston, IL: Northwestern University, Institute for the Learning Sciences.

Schiefele, U. (1992). Topic interest and levels of text comprehension. In K. A. Renninger, S. Hidi, & A. Krapp (Eds.), *The role of interest in learning and development* (pp. 151–182). Hillsdale, NJ: Lawrence Erlbaum Associates.

Schrum, L. (1995). Educators and the Internet: A case study of professional development. *Computers and Education, 24,* 221–228.

Scott, T., Cole, M., & Engel, M. (1992). Computers and education: A cultural constructivist perspective. In G. Grant (Ed.), *Review of Research in Education* (Vol. 18, pp. 191–251). Washington, DC: American Educational Research Association.

Seabrook, J. (1995, October 16). Home on the net. *New Yorker,* 66, 68, 70, 72, 74, 76.

Shulman, L. S. (1986). Those who understand: Knowledge growth in teaching. *Educational Researcher, 15,* 4–14.

Shulman, L. S. (1992). Toward a pedagogy of cases. In J. H. Shulman (Ed.), *Case methods in teacher education* (pp. 1–30). New York: Teachers College Press.

Smith, F. (1986). *Insult to intelligence: The bureaucratic invasion of our classrooms.* Portsmouth, NH: Heinemann.

Smith, M. L. (1987). Publishing qualitative research. *American Educational Research Journal, 24,* 173–183.

Snow, C. E. (1992). Perspectives on second-language development: Implications for bilingual education. *Educational Researcher, 21,* 16–19.

Spoehr, K. T., & Spoehr, L. W. (1994). Learning to think historically. *Educational Psychologist, 29,* 71–77.

Spring, J. (1994). *Deculturalization and the struggle for equality.* New York: McGraw-Hill.

Stahl, G., Sumner, T., & Owen, R. (1995). Share globally, adapt locally: Software assistance to locate and tailor curriculum posted to the Internet. *Computers and Education, 24,* 237–246.

Stein, N. L., & Miller, C. A. (1991). I win—You lose: The development of argumentative thinking. In J. F. Voss, D. N. Perkins, & J. W. Segal (Eds.), *Informal reasoning and education* (pp. 265–290). Hillsdale, NJ: Lawrence Erlbaum Associates.

Sykes, G., & Bird, T. (1992). Teacher education and the case idea. In G. Grant (Ed.), *Review of Research in Education* (Vol. 18, pp. 457–521). Washington, DC: American Educational Research Association.

Tannen, D. (1989). *Talking voices: Repetition, dialogue, and imagery in conversational discourse.* Cambridge: Cambridge University Press.

Tannen, D. (1990). *You just don't understand: Women and men in conversation.* New York: William Morrow.

Tiffin, J., & Rajasingham, L. (1995). *In search of the virtual class: Education in an information society.* London: Routledge.

Toulmin, S. E. (1958). *The uses of argument.* Cambridge: Cambridge University Press.

Tuchman, B. W. (1981). *Practicing history.* New York: Ballantine.

Tyack, D., & Cuban, L. (1995). *Tinkering toward utopia: A century of public school reform.* Cambridge, MA: Harvard University Press.

Wade, S., Thompson, A., & Watkins, W. (1994). The role of belief systems in authors' and readers' constructions of texts. In R. Garner & P. A. Alexander (Eds.), *Beliefs about text and instruction with text* (pp. 265–293). Hillsdale, NJ: Lawrence Erlbaum Associates.

Wells, G., & Chang-Wells, G. L. (1992). *Constructing knowledge together: Classrooms as centers of inquiry and literacy.* Portsmouth, NH: Heinemann.

Wiesel, E. (1982). *Night.* New York: Bantam

Wilson, S. M. (1992). A case concerning content: Using case studies to teach about subject matter. In J. H. Shulman (Ed.), *Case methods in teacher education* (pp. 64–89). New York: Teachers College Press.

Zeichner, K. M. (1993). *Educating teachers for cultural diversity.* East Lansing: Michigan State University, National Center for Research on Teacher Learning.

# Author Index

# Subject Index